Francesco Grecucci

Windows 11
Tips & Solutions

Francesco Grecucci

Windows 11
Tips & Solutions

Windows 11 – Tips and Solutions
by Francesco Grecucci

Book Cover: GlowUp! Design

ISBN: 9798314509418

Microsoft releases different versions of Windows 11. Some procedures may have undergone graphical or functional changes.

© 2025 – Francesco Grecucci
First Edition: April 2025

The First Edition was released in Italy in January 2025.
Original Title: Windows 11 Guide e Soluzioni

Summary

Written with love in Italy.

Preface

When Windows 10 was released, it was considered the "ultimate Windows": in other words, the latest chapter in the Redmond OS saga.

No longer a simple product, but a service, according to the concept of **Windows as a Service**, with updates and new versions distributed over time. The future seemed already written out.

A press release from Microsoft in 2021 revealed a major overhaul of Windows, known as Sun Valley. During the opening keynote of Microsoft Build 2021, Microsoft CEO Satya Nadella had referred to Sun Valley as "next generation Windows", without ever explicitly mentioning Windows 10, but simply talking about Windows.

And so, after a series of beta versions (not final but available for testers and developers) and numerous indiscretions, Windows 11 was released in October 2021.

What happened to the concept of Windows as a Service? And the "ultimate Windows"? Well, only fools never change their minds...

However, the spread of Windows 11 has been slow, with a not particularly positive trend. According to a report by Statcounter, in 2024 Windows 11 reached only 31.62% of the market share, against about 64% of Windows 10.

This slowdown is partly due to the poor reception received, in particular for:
- A graphical interface that has been criticized for the lack of some features present in Windows 10.
- Poor compatibility with PCs produced before 2018, which excluded a large portion of users.

Introduction

The more experienced users will want to forgive me for my perhaps excessive examples and for the rather quick and direct language. This is a practical manual, and I know what it feels like to panic just because of a Word file that won't open. I know how bad it is not to know where a connection or program is located in the moment of need. And, finally, I understand very well the feeling that occurs when you are in front of a totally different operating system than the previous one, without having any support points.

I was born on February 2000, a few days before the release of Windows 2000. I started playing with PCs that I was quite small and I used Windows XP for years. In about 2007, I switched to Vista and a couple of years later to 7. I had for a short time Windows 8 and for an already quite experienced (and modest, let's face it) user like me was a trauma. Then, finally, here I am with Windows 11. In the meantime, I developed a passion for retro computing and had the honor of discovering systems prior to my birth. In 2008 I got a notebook that made me rediscover Windows 98, seen few times on some of my father's customers' PCs. Later, in 2016, I started a small collection starting from Windows 3.1. In the same year I founded my website, starting from trending topics like Windows 10 and Arduino. Nowadays, I work as a SAP consultant and software developer in Italy.

The way Microsoft changes things can be frightening. Millions of users desperate just because the start menu has disappeared, leaving in its place a huge screen made up of colored blocks. You do not play with the habits of users!

In this book, I aim to explore some of the unique features of Windows 11 while incorporating several guides originally published on my now-offline blog. I have revisited my 2018 Windows 10 Tips and Solutions (Italian edition) and completely overhauled it—not just updating procedures for Microsoft's latest operating system, but expanding it by over 150 pages with new features, insights, curiosities, and a wealth of fresh tips and tricks for your PC.
I hope these pages prove useful and mark the beginning of a series of increasingly detailed manuals.

Book's Structure

Since this text is intended for all the users who will use Windows 11, whether they want to solve problems of the last minute or want to discover some secrets, it is divided in such a way as to cover different areas:

- The first section focuses on the main tools used in Microsoft operating systems and some basic concepts.
- The second section focuses on the features of the operating system, particularly the new settings panel. This topic is very important because many procedures start from there. We will also discuss Copilot, the new Start menu, and the highly useful Power User menu.
- The third part is dedicated to guides for everyday users. Simple things like finding features that seem to have disappeared with the new operating system, using the new Edge browser, solving problems with larger fonts... and much more to improve the user experience.
- The fourth part is for technicians and so-called geeks. There are plenty of guides that go down more in the heart of Windows 11 and also allow you to solve problems not really trivial.
- The last part is about the famous Tips & Tricks, designed for those who want to save time and impress friends during work breaks.

All will be interspersed with pleasant pills of history of Windows systems and computer science in general.

How to read this book

This is a manual, a manual to browse through, to hold in your hands on a bench and act like a *geek* or to use at work. But, most importantly, it can be read in any way. The first three sections are mostly easy to read, while the rest can be read as needed or in skips. Therefore, complete freedom, also thanks to a very direct and synthetic index.

Its task is to help you and accompany you, to be scribbled, highlighted and full of bookmarks on the corners of the pages, so that you can consult it easily *in case of need*.

Suggestions and corrections

Windows 11 is a software and is therefore dynamic. There will be news, new problems and so on. If you want to suggest something to me or correct correct some of my mistakes (after all, in life we are all a bit 'beta tester) you can write to me by email at grecucci.francesco@gmail.com.

Technical Characteristics

Operating system	Windows 11 Pro **24H2**
Language	English (United Kingdom)

> ▶ Some terms, like Personalise and Customise, are influenced by the UK version of Windows 11.
> ▶ Some tips may change in future versions of Windows 11.

Basic Elements

Key Aspects of Microsoft Windows

Precautions

Always keep in mind that anything you modify or, even worse, delete from your computer can cause **permanent damage**. This chapter contains the basic elements of Windows operating systems that will often be discussed in the following pages. Always remember to follow the procedures and **make backup copies of your data** (backups). If you are an aspiring computer technician, consider using a virtual machine or another computer to do all the experiments you want.

If you do not have administrator rights in the PC on which you are working, act only with prior permission of the person responsible.

Virtual Machines

You can use a virtual machine to play around with settings without damaging your PC. Many software such as VMware and Parallels Desktop are paid and for professional users. For those who, on the other hand, want something free, Oracle VM VirtualBox is available online.

A virtual machine is nothing more than an all-round emulation of a PC. All versions of Windows and Linux can be installed in it. Of course, the Host PC (the one that hosts the virtual machine) must have the necessary hardware requirements to hold the load of another operating system running.

You will have at your disposal one or more virtual disks in a file not accessible directly from the PC Host (therefore, the risk is really minimal) and an interface ready for use where to manage the various virtual environments. You can install Windows or Linux as if it were a real PC.

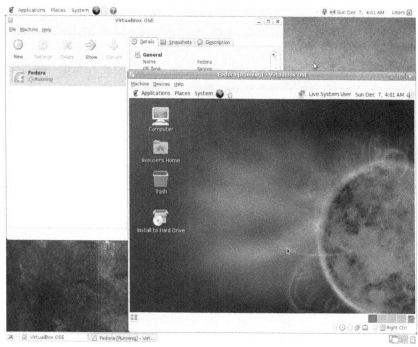

1 VirtualBox running on Linux with another Linux system.

What is an Operating System?

An operating system is a set of software that collaborate with each other to provide the user with an environment for interaction between hardware and software. Examples of operating systems are:

- **Windows**: produced by Microsoft and sold as a PC operating system, is one of the most popular operating systems.
- **macOS**: produced by Apple, is only available on its own devices.
- **Linux**: includes a family of open-source operating systems based on the Linux kernel, distributed according to the open source philosophy.

Open Source
Computer software is written in code according to a programming language. There are organizations made up of programmers who write and make the code free, making their work accessible to everyone and available for free.

Examples of open source software are: Mozilla Firefox, OpenOffice, LibreOffice, Blender, 7-ZIP, SuiteCRM.

Some operating systems: Linux Ubuntu, Linux Mint, OpenSUSE, Arch Linux.

File extensions

The files are identified by a name and an extension. For example, a photo might be called DOG.JPG, where DOG is the name and JPG is the extension.

A file extension indicates the **type of content** and allows the operating system to associate the file with the correct program in order to open or modify it. For example, DOG.JPG and MYSONG.MP3 are different files: the first one is a photograph, while the second one is a music track, and will be managed by programs specific to each type of file.

▶ Most common used file extensions

File Type	Extension
Unformatted text file (plain text without graphics)	.txt
Audio Files	.mp3
	.wav
	.ogg
Photos and Bitmap Images	.png
	.jpg
	.jpeg
	.bmp
	.gif
Videos	.avi
	.mpeg
	.wmv
	.mp4
	.3gp
	.flv
Windows Applications	.exe
Web Pages	.htm, .htm
Microsoft Word Documents	.doc
	.docx

Microsoft Excel Spreadsheets	.xls
	.xlsx
Microsoft PowerPoint Slideshow	.ppt
	.pptx
PDF Document	.pdf
Open Source WritingDocument	.odt
Open Source Spreadsheets	.ods
Open Source Slideshows	.odp
Compressed Files	.zip
	.rar

A file is a set of data such as a letter, excel sheet, song or image. An application is a set of instructions for the computer that process specific tasks. Applications or programs can be: Word, Excel, Google Chrome, etc.

User Interfaces Fundamentals

The user interface (UI) refers to the part of the operating system or software with which the end user interacts.

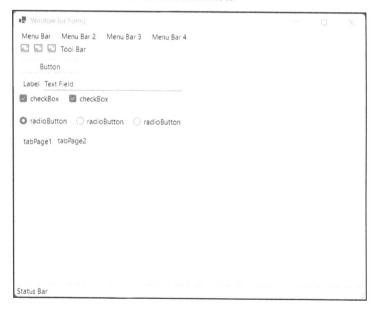

2 Some elements of a basic User Interface on Windows 11

- **Form or Window:** is a smaller portion of the entire area occupied by the operating system.

- **Menu Bar:** bar containing several context menus that can be clicked and within them are contained various operations.
- **Toolbar:** a set of icons to allow different actions to be performed.
- **Button:** by clicking on a button, the program will perform an action.
- **Text box:** allows the user to insert text, numbers, etc..
- **Label:** display text on screen, usually used to explain the function of a text box or other.
- **Check box:** allows you to check one or more options.
- **Radio Button:** allows you to tick only one of a number of options.
- **Tabs:** allow users to split the screen into several parts.

Do you know why they are called radio buttons?
In the past, cassette players made it possible to select the various functions (play, fast forward, back, record) one at a time. Pressing one button would cancel the previous selection. Radio buttons emulate this type of behavior by giving the user the option to choose one option at a time.

Here are the basic elements of the graphical interface of Windows.

- **Desktop:** main area and background screen of applications.
- **Icons:** represent files and applications in the form of small, easily recognisable graphics.
- **Taskbar:** contains the start menu (which is, the main menu that will be discussed in the following pages), shortcuts to the user's favorite applications, status and notification icons, time and date.

3 Desktop

Keyboard

A computer keyboard allows you to type not only letters and numbers, but also to give specific commands to your computer and use shortcuts for actions you would typically perform with a mouse. There are different system keys, such as:

4 Keyboard

1. **Shift** – Types capital letters and special characters when used with other keys.
2. **Caps Lock** – Toggles uppercase and lowercase typing.
3. **Ctrl (Control)** – Executes keyboard shortcuts.
4. **Alt** – Works with other keys for specific commands.
5. **Windows** – Opens the Start menu. used with other keys for shortcuts.
6. **Menu** – Functions like the right mouse button, opening context menus.
7. **Esc (Escape)** – Exits, cancels, or closes operations, menus, or dialogs.
8. **Function Keys (F1–F12)** – Serve as shortcuts for various functions, depending on the system or software. For example, pressing SHIFT + F12 in Microsoft Word saves your document without needing to use the mouse.

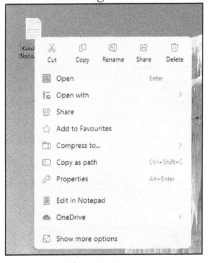

5 A context menu

There are also other system keys on keyboards. Usually on the right side between the QWERTY keyboard and the numeric keypad, but on notebooks or compact keyboards you can find them everywhere.

1. **Ins (Insert)** - enables or disables the insert/overwrite mode. In short, if you type a new word before another one, it replaces the already existing ones. By reactivating the Ins mode, new words are added to existing ones.
2. **Del/Delete** - delete the character to the right of the text cursor.

What is a text cursor?
The text cursor is that vertical hyphen in writing phase that indicates the point from which the characters will be typed.

3. **Prtscr -** takes a screenshot.
4. **Home** **-** moves the text cursor to the beginning of a document.
5. **End -** move the text cursor to the end of a document.
6. **Pg Up (Page Up) -** scrolls upwards in a document or web page.
7. **Pg Dn (Page Down) -** scrolls down a document or web page.
8. **Scroll Lock** – Originally designed to lock the cursor's position in spreadsheets. When enabled, it allows scrolling the entire sheet instead of moving the cursor. It is also used in the command prompt to pause output, preventing it from scrolling too fast and making it hard to read. It was commonly used in the MS-DOS era (1980s).
9. **Pause/Break:** is used to temporarily stop or terminate the execution of programs or processes in some environments, always MS-DOS or at least old.
10. **Num Lock:** activates or deactivates the numeric keypad which, if deactivated, becomes a set of arrow keys.

Task Manager

The Task Manager, was introduced many years ago in the Windows NT world: an environment unknown to home users, built on performance-hungry systems, and based on the same foundations that are present in today's Windows systems. In 2000, with the achievement of optimal performance by everyday PCs, NT became Windows 2000, which later evolved into XP. The distinction between home and business users was no longer as clear-cut as in the '90s, since both categories only differed by the version purchased, not by the entire software. With Windows XP, in 2002, Ctrl + Alt + Del gave rise to something more than a simple list of running programs. It evolved into a more powerful tool, providing a snapshot of both processes (programs running in memory) and CPU and RAM usage.

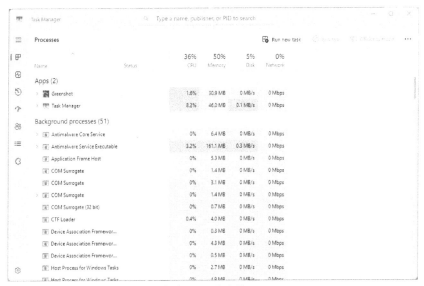

6 Windows 11 Task Manager

Inside the task manager

In Windows 11 you have a mature and graphically pleasing task manager which has several tabs.

- **Processes:** shows the running processes, related to the respective clearly displayed consumption of CPU, RAM, Disk Drive and GPU (video card).
- **Performance:** provides a graphical view of the use of the components mentioned in the previous point.

- **App History:** is a panel that shows the resource usage in the last month by different applications.
- **Startup Apps:** lists and manages the programs that run when the computer starts.
- **Users:** lists users currently connected to the PC.
- **Details:** lists the processes shown in detail with executable file name and unique PID identifier.
- **Services:** collects services: programs that perform specific tasks without user intervention. In short, they work silently in the background (but still consume valuable resources).

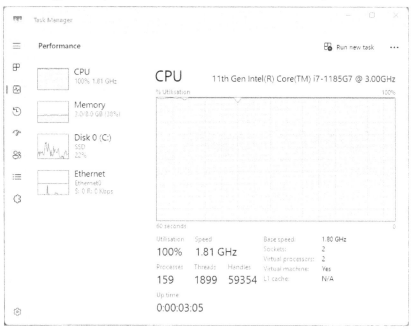

7 Performance View on Task Manager

You can open Task Manager in four ways:

1. Simultaneously pressing **CTRL + ALT + DELETE** on the PC keyboard and choosing the Task Manager entry in the screen that appears.
2. Pressing **CTRL + SHIFT + ESC** simultaneously on the keyboard.
3. By right clicking on the start menu (Power User Menu) and choosing the item **Task Manager**.
4. By right-clicking on the taskbar and selecting **Task Manager**.

File Extensions

Windows has numerous file extensions, each specifying an important parameter: **the program used to open the file**. Every file is a collection of different types of information. There is no single program that can open all types, but each format is associated with a specific program for opening it. Once the association is created, the file will have an icon related to its type and can be opened by the associated application.

However, there are file types that are not data files and cannot be opened by an app because they are programs themselves. It would be unthinkable to encounter an error such as *I can't open this program with any application*. **Therefore, there are system extensions that serve specific functions.**

System File Extensions

Below are the main system extensions in Windows.

Libraries and Executables

- **.EXE**: this extension stands for executable, the most important and used type of executable file. Every application is an executable.
- **.COM**: rarely used nowadays. It contains 16 bit instructions made for the old DOS systems.
- **.BIN**: a .bin file is a binary file that contains data in a format readable by a specific program, often used for software installation or disk images.
- **BAT**: it functions as both an executable file and a data file. It is a set of commands, a script—similar to those run from the *Run* window—written in a language called Batch (which we will explore in the section related to the Command Prompt) and then **executed**.

- **.DLL: Dynamic Link Libraries**: they are not standalone programs, but contain similar types of information. The difference between an executable file and a library is that a DLL cannot be run on its own. It is always linked to another software that utilizes its resources.

Configuration Files

Configuration files are used to define the parameters of a program or video game. In the old video game DOOM, released 25 years ago, there was a small file with the **.CFG** extension that contained all the settings: audio card, keyboard commands, etc. It was not manually written; instead, it was generated by a program based on the player's choices. Configuration files should only be modified directly in special cases. Nowadays, more modern formats than the old **.cfg, .ini, .conf, .txt** are used, or the parameters are directly inserted into the system registry (which we will explore later in this book).

System Files

System files, known by the .sys extension, contain hardware configurations and driver settings.

8 A Log File.

Log Files

Log files are essential for troubleshooting software issues. Every well-designed program always writes a chronological list of events in a text file with the extension **.log**. For example, the Mozilla Firefox log file can be helpful if it crashes (it closes suddenly) in identifying the cause of the problem.

Microsoft Management Console (MMC) Files

Files with extension **.mmc** are components of the Microsoft Management Console, which we will talk about in the section related to the Administration Tools.

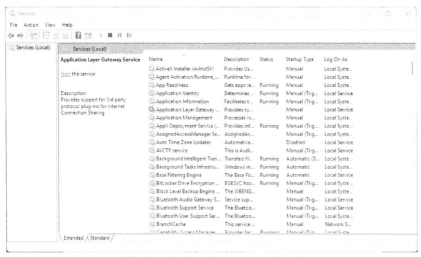

9 Windows Services Management Console

Text files and formatted files

The simplest type of data file is a purely textual one. Just open the Notepad (the basic text editor), write something and save the file with extension **.txt.** These are processed as plain text format files, such as . bat, source codes . c, . cpp, . py, . php, . js, web pages. html, web scripts. php, . js and many more. **However, there are programs that generate files with additional formatting, known as formatted files.** Formatting defines the style and visual appearance of a file, such as in the case of a Word document. If we tried to open a Word document in Notepad, we'd see a series of unintelligible characters. These are documents formatted and/or encoded for that specific application, which cannot be read as plain text.

What is a source code?
The same goes for **programs**. They are files containg compiled instructions that are translated into a format the computer understands. Only the **source code**, written by the developer before passing to the compiler, is understandable by humans to the programming languages, not the computer.

Windows Tools

Windows Tools are a set of system utilities that allow you to change various settings, particularly in the areas of security and disk management. The folder can be found within the Start menu. Below are the most commonly used tools:

- **System Configuration:** often known as MSCONFIG within the Run window, it is used to define the boot settings of the operating system.
- **Local Security Policy:** contains security settings (such as password validity), primarily related to corporate network with domains.
- **Windows Memory Diagnostic:** restarts the PC and runs a utility to check the health of the RAM.
- **Computer Management:** contains many system utilities, including:
  - **Shared folders:** allows you to manage folders shared on the network with other PCs.
  - **Local users and groups:** manage users and groups, including system ones.
  - **Disk Management:** allows you to manage all the disk drives installed in your computer.
- **Services:** a panel for managing system services. Each service can be started automatically (on startup) or manually (when called by a program). A third option allows you to disable it completely. We will see in the next paragraph.
- **Event viewer:** displays detailed logs of events from the operating system and applications.

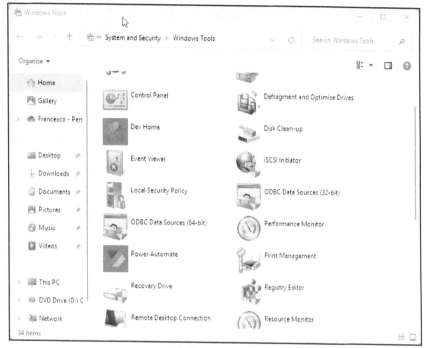

10 Windows Tools Window.

Most of these are modules in the Microsoft Management Console, a hub that collects advanced system settings.

Services

Let's look at the term **Service** in Windows. This term will be used in more advanced procedures throughout this text and may appear in web troubleshooting guides. **A service is a software application that operates in the background, without user interaction, often running unnoticed, providing specific functionalities.** These can start automatically when Windows starts or be called up manually.

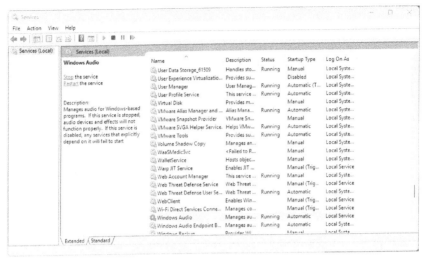

11 Services Window

Features such as network connection, printer management or tasks like automatic backups are possible thanks to the services.

Managing services is usually done by technicians and programmers. However, during troubleshooting, you may need to turn them off or reboot them in order to find any problems that may be caused by them.

Custom Services

Services are not only made by Microsoft. Different programs can install services and provide features such as servers, background functionality, and so on. An example of a custom service is MYSQL. In a few words, it runs on Windows startup a database server. You can access the database by just pressing your start button and a few moments after Windows startup!

Less services...faster system!

On the internet, there are several guides that suggest to deactivate several Windows services to make your computer faster. Be careful, as I often say!

12 Windows Audio Properties (you can see this window by double-clicking a service in Power Tools > Services).

Command Prompt

Computers used to only accept text-based commands, in an interface called CLI or *command line interface*. The one we use now is the GUI or *Graphical User Interface*. However, textual instructions may still be necessary, especially in the case of advanced modifications or to use professional tools without a graphical interface. In Windows you don't need to exit the GUI and enter a full text session, but you use a window through which you can do everything: the command prompt.

You can find it in the Start menu within the Accessories folder or by right-clicking on the Start button or in the Run (Windows+R) command window, type CMD.

13 Command Prompt ready to dance!

It is also possible to run it as an administrator, with a high level of risk.

The command prompt (although it is still available for use and is still needed) has been largely replaced by the **PowerShell** console for most operations.

PowerShell

Microsoft introduced PowerShell, a new powerful command prompt. However, it can be uncomfortable when used as a full replacement for the classic prompt, since it accepts different instructions than the traditional command prompt. It should not be underestimated, especially because there are many procedures written exclusively for PowerShell.

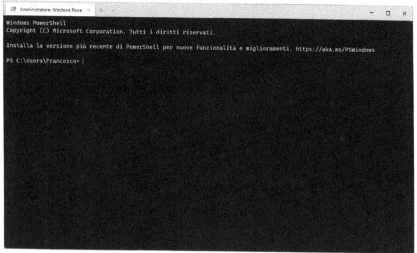

14 It looks very similar to the classic prompt, but it is not so..

PowerShell may be slower than the classic command prompt (CMD) for a number of reasons related to its architecture and advanced features. **We'll go into Powershell later in this book.**

Batch Language

The prompt has predefined commands that allow for folder navigation and instruction modification. Put together in a file with the .bat extension and create a real program. If applications are installed that accept commands via the prompt, it is possible to create automation codes called scripts.

For example, if we have a program that can be run in a particular mode through special parameters of the prompt, you can double click on a batch script to avoid writing everything every time. Here is a demonstration:

```
c:\program files\program\app.exe /d /f
```

This string does nothing but call the executable file and issue boot commands. You can write all to a .bat file and launch the program in mode /d and /f with a double click on the icon just created.

15 File batch icon: simply double click!

Device Manager

"In 1998, setting up a printer required a degree from Stanford and a couple of weeks away from the outside world. The headaches were quite intense and many technicians decided to take baths in a fairy lake to dissolve the spells caused by evil spirits called <u>drivers</u>."

Fairy tales aside, drivers have always been a problem. But what are they? You may have heard about it, maybe around or from someone who has said the phrase *"Did you install the drivers?"*. Drivers are nothing more than the software part that allows interaction between the PC and the device. For example, the mouse driver allows communication between the PC and the mouse, performing a coordinate calculation to ensure the cursor movement on the screen. As well as the printer will pass all the document to be printed to the device, receiving in response from it information about the status of ink and paper or a possible paper jam.

Drivers are nothing more than software and as such can be installed and removed. In addition, unfortunately, they may have malfunctions and bugs, for which you may need to upgrade them to a later version. There is a Windows module called **Device Manager**. It lists all the devices connected to the computer, both **internal** and **external**. You can easily reach it by right clicking on the Start button.

In a desktop PC, the screen, mouse and keyboard are examples of **external** peripherals. A hard disk, the video card are examples of **internal** peripherals, that is installed inside the computer.

If we talk about a laptop, the **keyboard** and **trackpad** (the built-in mouse of the notebook) are also internal peripherals.

16 Internal vs External Peripherals

▶ **How to open Device Manager:**

1. Open the Power User Menu (Windows + X key combination or right-click on start button)
2. Click on Device Manager.

Device Manager is very useful, as you will see in the next section, but like any Windows feature for advanced users, it carries risks. If you don't know where to put your hands, you may cause problems with your PC, until it becomes unusable.

17 Power User Menu

Device manager divides all devices into categories. Right-clicking a component allows you to update its drivers, temporarily deactivate the device or completely uninstall it. Driver updates can be done from the Microsoft database, by downloading packages directly from the manufacturer's website or with the CD provided inside the original packaging.

You can also view the information and perform other operations by clicking on the Properties button, in which the various errors or problems encountered by the operating system itself are often indicated in case of a driver malfunction or failed configuration.

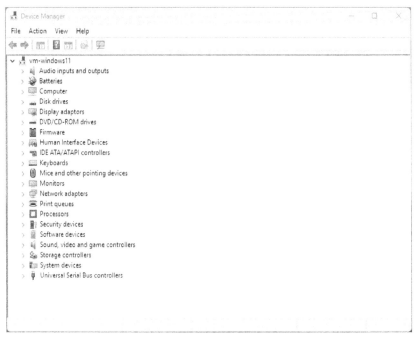

18 Device Manager

System32 and SysWOW64

The system files are contained in the folder C:\Windows. The files that make up the Windows system, are instead located in the paths C:\Windows\System32 and C:\Windows\SysWOW64.

For the two architectures (32 and 64 bit), respectively, the two folders will contain the drivers and basic elements for operating the operating system.

The difference between 32 bit and 64 bit architecture

When we talk about 32 bit and 64 bit we are referring to a property that concerns both the hardware and the software. Both are *architectures* and are nothing more than two ways of handling information by the CPU of any device. Once upon a time (and even today, in microcontrollers like Arduino) there were 8-bit and 16-bit architectures. These values define the size of a simple variable within a hardware system, the size of a CPU's internal registers (which are the containers for variables inside the processor) and the sizes of the component buses (for data and addresses). This means that the more data you can accumulate in a given time, the better performance you will have. For example, an 8-bit variable may contain a maximum number of $2^8 = 256$ binary values (max 11111111 = 255 because 0 is the first value).

> A variable is an area of memory to hold data.

▶ Knowing RAM (Random Access Memory)

> **RAM** is a temporary, fast and random-access memory that is used to hold running programs. When you launch an application, it is loaded from the disk (HD or SSD) into the RAM where it can run faster. The more RAM a PC has, the more applications it can run at once and the faster its operations.
>
> The RAM is volatile, that is, it loses data when the PC is turned off, since it only works thanks to the electric charge. For this, if the power goes off and you haven't saved your document, everything you were doing will be lost unless you have saved the file on a permanent memory device such as a hard disk.

Windows 11 does not support 32-bit architecture. The latest Microsoft operating system to provide such support is Windows 10. This type of architecture is now obsolete, in particular because of the technical limit on RAM. With a 32-bit system the maximum installed RAM limit is 4 GB. It is an outdated memory capacity (lately we start from 8GB up to reach 128GB on the most powerful systems). With 64 bit - if the CPU and components support this architecture - you can have up to **18.446.744.073.709.551.616** B or rather 16 Exabyte. However, no system currently supports this amount of memory. Below is a table showing the memory limits of the various editions of Windows 11.

Windows version	X64 max. supported	ARM64 max. supported
Windows 11 Education	2 TB	2 TB
Windows 11 Pro For Workstation	6 TB	6 TB
Windows 11 Pro	2 TB	2 TB
Windows 11 Home	128 GB	128 GB

▶ Comparison with older versions

Windows version	Max. supported
Windows 10 Home (64 bit)	128GB
Windows 10 Pro (64 bit)	512GB
Windows 10 Enterprise (64 bit)	512GB
Windows 8.1 (64 bit)	192GB
Windows 8.1 Pro (64 bit)	512GB
Windows 7 Starter (32 bit)	2GB
Windows 7 Home Basic (64 bit)	8GB
Windows 7 Home Premium (64 bit)	16GB
Windows 7 Professional (64 Bit)	192GB
Windows 7 Enterprise (64 Bit)	192GB
Windows Server 2016 Essentials	64GB
Windows Server 2012 Standard	24TB
Windows Server 2012 Datacenter	24TB

Wow! Who wouldn't like a PC with 24TB of RAM?! However, performance wouldn't be that excellent: you would just be able to run a large number of programs simultaneously. This is because RAM alone isn't enough; you also need a (or more) CPU and peripherals (hard disk, or preferably an SSD, graphics cards, etc.) of similar quality to the most powerful component. If not, there would be so-called bottlenecks.

Performance Bottleneck

I will use a metaphor to help you understand the concept of **bottleneck**: imagine driving on a highway where the limit is 200km/h for a 50km long stretch, and then arrive at a very slow-moving zone with a 20 km/h limit, losing all the benefits obtained from the previous stretch of road and arriving late.

A high-performance, state-of-the-art CPU paired with an 80GB hard drive from 2004 is an example of how reusing old components in a new PC can be inefficient. In fact, a poorly done upgrade can be an unnecessary expense and not give particular improvements in terms of performance. As well as 16GB of RAM and a video card with 16MB of graphics memory. Similar situations are to be avoided. It is very likely that the bottleneck already occurs by default for technical reasons, such as between RAM and hard disk due to their different operating speeds (the first one is an electronic memory, the second one an electromechanical type memory).

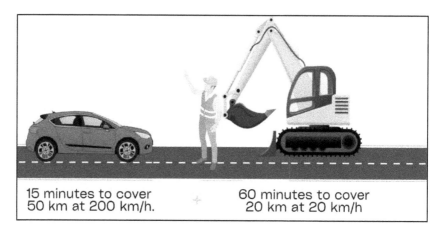

15 minutes to cover 50 km at 200 km/h.   60 minutes to cover 20 km at 20 km/h

New Features

News at a glance

Windows 11 includes several improvements and new features compared to its predecessor. Some of these are:

1. **New design:** With version 11, Windows adopts a new look, featuring a centered taskbar and more rounded, uniform icons. The user interface has been redesigned to simplify the use of the operating system and provide a more modern experience.

2. **New Start menu:** The Start menu in Windows 11 has been redesigned and now features larger, more spacious icons, with a section dedicated to recent apps and recently used files. You can also customize the Start menu to suit your needs.

3. **Improved Dark Mode:** Windows 11 introduces an enhanced Dark Mode. This mode is increasingly used because it reduces eye strain and makes text more legible.

4. **New animations:** Windows 11 introduces new animations to improve the user experience, such as window transitions and app previews in the taskbar.

5. **Microsoft Teams integration:** Windows 11 integrates Microsoft Teams directly into the operating system, allowing users to chat, make video calls, and collaborate within the OS.

6. **New Notification Center:** The Notification Center in Windows 11 has been redesigned and now features a cleaner, easier-to-use interface, with quick access to notifications, settings, and widgets.

7. **New widgets:** Windows 11 introduces a new customizable widget area, allowing users to view information such as news, weather, calendar, and more.

8. **Snap Layouts:** A new feature that allows you to organize open windows in various predefined configurations on the screen. This makes multitasking more efficient and helps you work with multiple applications open in an organized manner.

9. **New Microsoft Edge:** Windows 11 introduces a new version of the Edge browser, which features an improved user interface and new features, such as native support for extensions.

10. **Improved search:** The search feature in Windows 11 has been enhanced, allowing users to search for files, apps, and settings more efficiently.

11. **Gaming support:** Windows 11 introduces new gaming features, such as support for DirectX 12 Ultimate and integration with Xbox Game Pass, enabling users to access a vast library of games directly from their desktop.

12. **Performance improvements:** Windows 11 is designed to offer superior performance over Windows 10, thanks to enhancements in memory management, startup speed, and CPU/GPU optimization.

13. **Touch support:** Windows 11 is designed to work on touch-enabled devices, with new features such as support for touch gestures and optimization of the interface.

Compatibility Issues

Windows 11 is incompatible with many PCs, which has significantly slowed its adoption compared to Windows 10. Its requirements are more advanced and the TPM requirements have forced many users to hold back from upgrading.

Minimal requirements

The minimum requirements (which, remember, are the minimum necessary to allow the system to work but do not guarantee adequate performance) from the Microsoft site are as follows:

- **CPU (Central Processing Units):** 1 Ghz or faster with 2 or more cores and included in the list of approved CPUs. The processor in your PC will be a major determining factor for running Windows 11. The clock speed (the requirement of 1 GHz or faster) and the number of cores (2 or more) are inherent in the design of the processor and cannot be replaced or upgraded (in short, buy a new CPU if your motherboard allows it).

- **RAM:** 4 GB. It's the minimum necessary, but I recommend at least 8GB for a light use (internet, email, office) and at least 16GB for a more intense use. It is a more easily upgradable PC component and can be upgraded (for example, by purchasing another 4GB module in addition to the one already present).

- **Storage:** 64 GB storage device or larger. This requirement actually refers to the storage space needed for the operating system installation. However, such a small drive is useful if you do not need to save large amounts of data. Storage space is closely related to the memory requirements for the amount of data that will be saved. It is in any case an easily expandable and/or replaceable unit.

- **System Firmware:** UEFI (Unified Extensible Firmware Interface, a modern version of BIOS) with Secure Boot. This requirement is one of those that does not allow installation on systems with BIOS. Generally, PCs from 2010 onwards still have UEFI firmware

- **TPM:** Trusted Platform Module (TPM) version 2.0. If your device does not meet the minimum requirements due to TPM, it will not install. I will dedicate the next paragraph to the TPM.

- **Graphics card:** compatible with DirectX 12 or later with WDDM 2.0 driver.

- **Display:** High definition (720p) display larger than 9" in diagonal, 8 bits per color channel. If your screen size is less than 9", the Windows user interface may not be fully visible.

- **Internet connectivity and Microsoft accounts:** Windows 11 requires Internet connectivity and a Microsoft account to complete the device configuration at first use.

Discover the TPM (Trusted Platform Module)

The TPM (Trusted Platform Module) is a hardware chip built into many computers, designed to provide advanced security features. Its main purpose is to protect the operating system, data, and applications from external attacks. The TPM was developed by the Trusted Computing Group (TCG), an international consortium of leading technology companies, which has defined global standards for computer system security.

This chip offers numerous features, including:

- **Data encryption:** protects sensitive data by using secure stored cryptographic keys.
- **Security key management:** enables the generation and safe storage of private and certified keys.
- **Hardware identification:** provides a unique digital signature for the device, which is used to authenticate the hardware.
- **System boot protection:** ensures that the operating system is only booted with authorized software, preventing unauthorized changes to firmware or OS (Secure Boot).

In simple words, the TPM creates a secure environment for generating, managing and using encryption keys. This hardware environment is protected from software attacks, making it one of the most reliable security systems available on modern computers.

New features of the TPM in Windows 11

- **Advanced ransomware protection:** thanks to its integration with hardware encryption, the TPM works together with Windows Hello and BitLocker to protect your data even in case of ransomware attacks.
- **Pluton integration:** some modern devices include the Microsoft Pluton security processor, a TPM extension designed to further enhance device security. Pluton is integrated directly into the CPU, making it more difficult to compromise the chip.
- **Verification of the boot chain:** the TPM verifies that all components loaded during startup are authentic and have not been tampered with. In case of anomalies, the system can block the boot to protect the data.
- **Windows Defender Application Guard:** uses the TPM to create secure containers while browsing the web, protecting the system from malware and phishing.

▶ Compatibility with TPM 2.0

Windows 11 requires support for TPM 2.0 or higher. This standard, introduced in 2013, represents a significant improvement over TPM 1.2 by including:

- Improved compatibility with modern CPUs and operating systems.
- More secure encryption algorithms, such as SHA-256 and RSA-2048.

What is ransomware?

Ransomware is one of the worst threats to your PC's security, as it encrypts all the data on your computer and demands a ransom payment for their recovery. The ransom should not be paid, as in most cases, the data is not recovered.

To protect yourself from this type of infection, you need to use advanced protection systems such as the TPM and a reliable antivirus. In addition, it is essential to use common sense, checking the security of the websites you visit and avoiding downloads from unreliable sources.

Finally, it is always advisable to make regular backups of your data on external media, keeping them disconnected from the PC and away from the Internet. This way, in case of a ransomware attack, your important data will be safe and you can restore it without having to pay any unnecessary ransom.

There has been some criticism of Microsoft's decision to make TPM support mandatory for Windows 11. Some users see this as a way to force users to upgrade to new PCs or buy an external TPM chip. In addition, some security experts have pointed out that TPM may not be a perfect solution for PC security, as these chips can be vulnerable to certain types of attacks.

19 A TPM module.

Check your PC's compatibility with Windows 11

Before upgrading to Windows 11, you can download the **PC Health Check** tool. The latter only checks if the components in your PC are compatible.

1. You can download the tool at the following link: https://aka.ms/GetPCHealthCheckApp

2. Search within the start menu for the PC Health Check application and launch the tool.

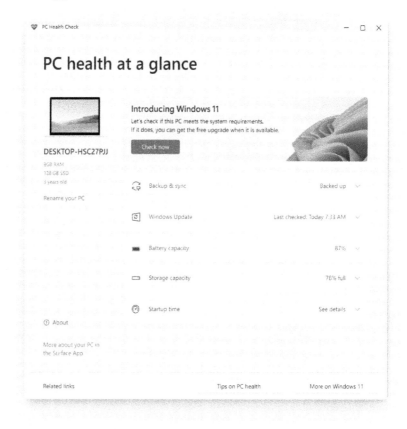

From which version of Windows 10 can I upgrade to 11?

Your device must be running Windows 10 version 2004 or later in order to upgrade through Windows Update. Free updates are available through Windows Update in **Settings** > **Windows Update**.

Start Menu

The start menu of Windows 11 is a bit different from its previous versions and from the traditional style we have been used to for over twenty years now.

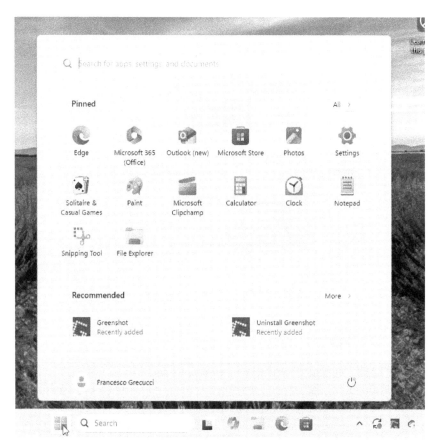

The screen consists of four basic elements:

- **Search box:** is useful for searching for files, documents and applications on your PC. It is also useful to search for settings: if, for example, I need to configure a bluetooth device, I just have to write *bluetooth* in it and the corresponding panel will appear among the results.
- **Pinned:** this section groups together some applications installed on the PC. You can pin your favorite apps here for quick access (in some versions of Windows it can be replaced by a list of favorite Apps).
- **More:** a button that opens a list of all installed applications.
- **Recommended Items:** lists the recently opened items.
- **User name:** by clicking on it you can open the user settings, block the session or disconnect the user.
- **Shutdown button:** allows you to shut down, restart, or put your PC to sleep.

The Windows button on your PC keyboard is identified by the Windows logo on the button placed, generally, between the Ctrl and Alt buttons) as shown in the images below:

Windows 10 style button
By LouisCYUL - Own work, CC BY-SA 4.0,
https://commons.wikimedia.org/w/index.php?curid=45634191

Windows 11 style button
By sonic exe - Own work, CC BY-SA 4.0,
https://commons.wikimedia.org/w/index.php?curid=113525394

What is the difference between Lock and Sign Out?

- The **Lock** command keeps all your programs open while protecting your PC from unauthorized access, leaving a screen, identical to the access one, that requires the entry of the password to return to use the system.

- The **Sign Out** command closes all applications and files, returning you to the login screen as if your PC had just been restarted.

How to place the start button on the left

Microsoft's decision to move the Start button and its icons to the center may be inconvenient for many users who have been accustomed to their original position for years. You can revert the icons to the left.

1. Right-click on the taskbar and click on Taskbar Settings.
2. Expand the box Taskbar Behaviours.
3. In the box next to the label Taskbar alignment choose Left.

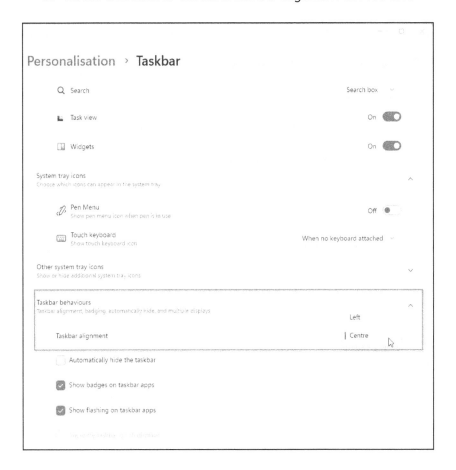

The power user menu

Earlier I mentioned about some components of Windows that can be accessed by right clicking on the Start button. This is possible with the **Power User Menu** context menu, which can also be opened using Windows + X buttons on the keyboard.

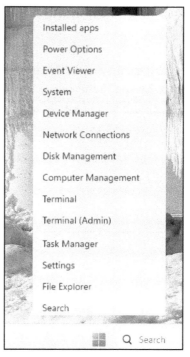

20 A secondary start menu, made of very useful shortcuts

- **Installed apps:** opens the settings section where you can see the programs installed on your PC, giving you the option to uninstall them.
- **Mobility Center:** groups various parameters and features for laptop owners such as brightness adjustment, volume, battery preset (energy saving, balanced, high performance), connection to a second screen and synchronization settings.
- **Power Options:** opens the settings section where you can manage screen off and standby.
- **Event Viewer:** shows the events from the operating system and applications in a detailed and ordered log.
- **System:** opens the window containing your PC's information and security status.

- **Device Manager:** shortcut to the device manager.
- **Network Connections:** opens the settings section dedicated to network connections (wi-fi, cable network, VPN networks, etc.).
- **Disk Management:** manages the mass storage disks installed in the PC.
- **Computer Management:** contains many system utilities including:
    - o **Shared Folders:** collects and manages folders shared on the network with other PCs.
    - o **Local users and groups:** contains users and groups, including system users.
    - o **Disk Management:** manages installed disk drives.
- **Terminal:** shortcut to cmd command, could be replaced by PowerShell.
- **Terminal (admin):** the prompt with administrator rights, could be replaced by PowerShell with administrator rights.
- **Task Manager:** opens Task Manager (one of many ways to do so...).
- **Settings:** opens the settings panel, I will talk about in the next pages.
- **File Explorer:** runs the Explorer (file and folder viewer).
- **Search:** opens the Windows 11 search screen.
- **Run:** I think you know it very well, but I will repeat it again: it is used to start programs and execute commands quickly.
- **Shut Down or Sign Out**
    - o Log out.
    - o Sleep (Stand-By).
    - o Shuts down the system (turns off).
    - o Restart the system.
- **Desktop:** shows the desktop and hides the currently featured applications.

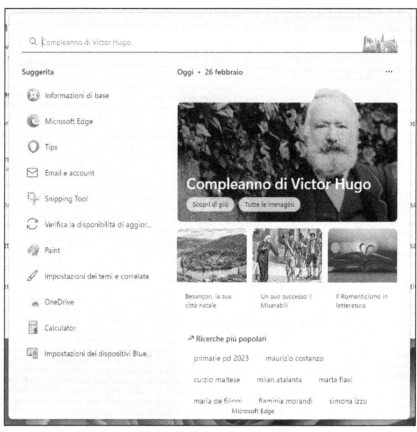

21 Windows's search window.

The new File Explorer

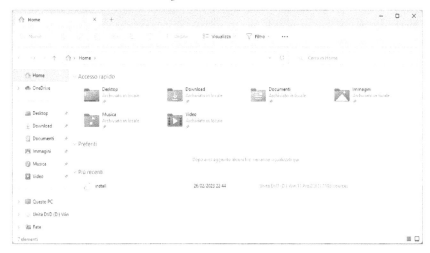

A very important change in Windows 11 is the new version of Windows Explorer.

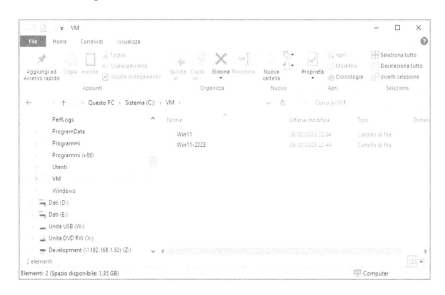

22 The previous File Explorer (Windows 10)

In addition to a change of icons and the general appearance, the new File Explorer has a very practical function: **tab navigation**.

It no longer makes it necessary to open multiple windows if you work on multiple folders, but allows you to work in portions of the same window, called tabs.

How do you do it? Just click on the ＋ button next to the last tab or use the keyboard shortcut CTRL + T.

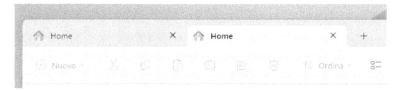

This solution not only allows a more convenient organization for the user but makes File Explorer faster and more efficient by not having to create multiple windows.

File Explorer Views

By clicking on the View button, you can set different file and folder views within the File Explorer screen, including:

- **Extra Large Icons:** displays icons and file thumbnails in large format, ideal for containing photos.

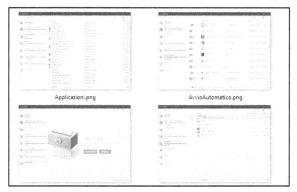

- **Large Icons:** displays icons and file previews in a smaller size.

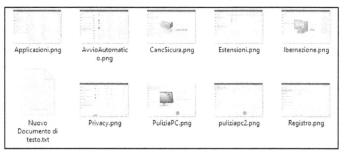

- **Medium-sized icons:** standard icon view.

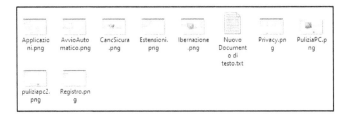

- **Small Icons:** thumbnails are hidden and only icons are present. Ideal for folders containing many files.

- **List:** display list of files in the folder.

- **Details:** one of the most useful views in Windows. It allows you to show various file details and sort them according to them.

You can add additional details by right-clicking on the column header.

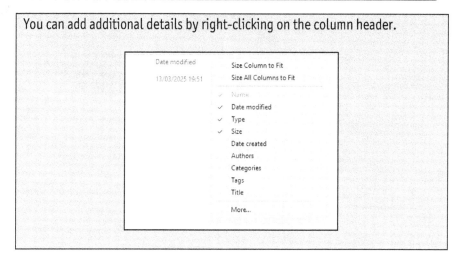

- **Tiles**: shows files in large tiles with a small preview, the file type and size.

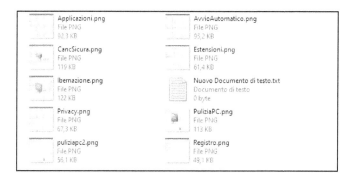

- **Content:** a hybrid between the detail view and large icons.

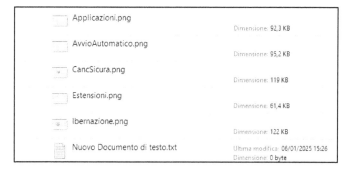

New context menu and the "show more options"

A change that wasn't well received, especially initially, is the modification of context menus in Windows 11 compared to previous versions. The menus have been reorganized, but you can return to the traditional view by clicking **Show more options**.

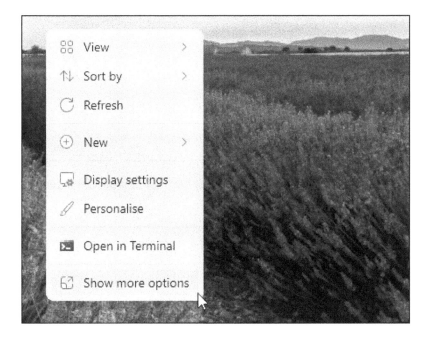

Settings

The most controversial feature added in Windows 10 was the replacement of the Control Panel, which remains accessible through the search in the **Search** box of the taskbar, with the new **Settings** panel.

23 Search Box inside the taskbar

In Windows 11, this comes with a completely renewed graphic interface and a more intuitive view. The integrated search box greatly simplifies troubleshooting and finding settings panels.

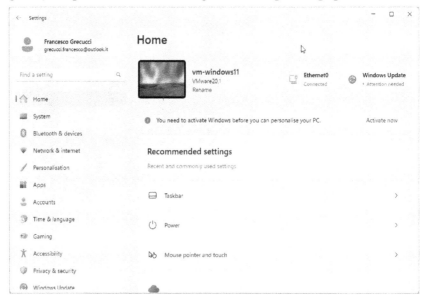

24 Settings Panel in Windows 11

The developers have decided to group the entries of the new Settings panel into these categories:

- **System:** general system settings and basic peripherals.
    - **Display:** manages the settings of the screen (resolution, text size) and any other monitors or projectors connected. In addition, from here you can set the night mode and possible activation/deactivation times.

- **Sound:** manages the sound card and playback devices. Helps configure the microphone and volume levels of various incoming and outgoing applications,
- **Notifications:** Manage notifications and related panel (bottom right of screen).
- **Focus:** activates a mode to promote concentration during time-based sessions. It allows to show a timer for the duration of the session, hide incoming notifications etc.
- **Power:** you can set screen off and standby, define energy saver options, etc.
- **Storage:** manages disk space locally and allows the activation of the *Storage Sense* function, in which Windows automatically frees disk space by deleting unnecessary files (temporary files, recycle bin),
- **Nearby sharing:** share files, photos and links with nearby devices.
- **Multi-tasking:** allows you to change the display settings and manage windows in multitasking even on multiple screens.
- **For developers:** allow users to enable developer mode, access advanced debugging tools, manage file extensions, configure remote device connections, and tweak other settings for development tasks. This section helps developers streamline their workflow when building, testing, and deploying applications.
- **Activation:** allows you to monitor the status of your Windows license in use.
- **Troubleshoot:** manages the settings for the troubleshooting tool.
- **Recovery:** allows you to reset your PC to its original settings in case of problems or restart it in troubleshooting mode.
- **Projecting to this PC:** in case the PC supports Miracast, you can project content from another computer or an Android smartphone on its screen.
- **Remote Desktop:** shows the settings of the Remote Desktop client, which allows you to remotely control your PC simply by entering its network name.

- **Clipboard:** allows you to manage settings on the clipboard, such as the clipboard history. This history allows you to save recent clipboard contents, that is everything that you copy and then go to paste.
- **System Components:** allows you to manage the system components that are preinstalled in Windows like Microsoft Store or Game Bar.
- **Optional Features:** shows and allows adding optional features on your operating system like OpenSSH Client, supplemental fonts, Wireless display, etc.
- **About:** opens the Windows window containing your PC information and security status.

- **Bluetooth and Devices:** manages peripherals connected to the PC via cable, Wi-Fi or Bluetooth. It replaced the old Windows 7 Devices and Printers.
  - **Devices:** manages the connection of Bluetooth peripherals and other connected devices.
  - **Printers & Scanners:** the printer management panel where new printers can be managed and configured.
  - **Mobile devices:** allows you to connect an Android smartphone.
  - **Cameras:** manages the cameras installed in the local network or on the PC.
  - **Mouse:** the mouse settings, such as the main button (in case the user is left-handed), the speed of the scroll wheel etc.
  - **Pen & Windows Ink:** settings for handwriting recognition in the case of tactile use.
  - **AutoPlay:** sets the command to be executed when connecting a removable device (USB stick, memory card, CD).
  - **USB:** allows you to manage notifications for USB devices issues.

- **Network & Internet:** is the new hub for networking and sharing.
  - **Wi-Fi:** Manage Wi-Fi connections and networks.
  - **Ethernet:** View and configure wired connections.
  - **Dial-up:** Configure dial-up connections.

- **Mobile Hotspot:** Share your Internet connection with other devices.
- **VPN:** Configure and manage VPN connections.
- **Proxy:** Set the proxy server to connect to the Internet.
- **Advanced Network Settings:** Change the advanced network settings, such as advanced sharing settings, data usage, hardware and connection properties and network reset.

> Network Settings may change because of the networking devices installed in your PC.

- **Personalisation:** groups the settings about colors and backgrounds to be used both in the desktop environment and on the lock screen.
    - **Background:** allows you to change the desktop background, it is also possible to take images to change at defined time intervals.
    - **Colours:** provides a color palette for various Windows elements. You can also switch between light and dark themes in apps.
    - **Themes:** is a set of preset backgrounds, colors, sounds and pointers. You can also add them from the Windows Store.
    - **Dynamic Lighting:** is a feature that allows users to customize and synchronize the RGB lighting on their connected devices, like keyboards, mice, and other peripherals. Instead of using third-party software provided by device manufacturers, Windows itself can control the lighting settings for supported hardware. With Dynamic Lighting, you can change colors, patterns, and effects in a simple and unified way directly from the Windows Settings menu. It provides a more seamless experience for gamers, content creators, or anyone who enjoys personalizing their setup.
    - **Lock screen:** allows you to change the lock screen background and choose Apps to display a summary (like a smartphone's lock screen).

- **Text Input:** Text input settings in Windows 11 control how your device handles typing and input across the system. This includes preferences for typing, spell-checking, predictive text, and on-screen keyboards.
- **Start:** brings together the Start menu settings.
- **Taskbar:** collects the typical settings on the taskbar.
- **Fonts:** shows the list of fonts installed on your system. You can download more from the Store.
- **Device Usage:** the Device Usage section in Windows 11 settings allows you to personalize your device based on how you primarily use it. It provides options to let Windows suggest tailored features, tools, and services depending on your preferences.

- **App:** allows you to manage installed apps (including desktop apps, which are the traditional programs for Windows).
  - **Installed Apps:** here you can manage, repair and uninstall programs.
  - **Advanced App Settings:** configure app permissions, manage app data sharing, and toggle features like archiving unused apps.
  - **Default Apps:** lets you choose which apps to use to open web pages, emails, multimedia files, etc.
  - **Offline Maps:** manages offline map downloads so you always have them at hand, even when there is no Internet connection.
  - **Apps for Websites:** you can remove the association of a website with the installed app.
  - **Video playback:** combines settings for movie playback with apps that integrate with Windows 11.
  - **Startup:** manages the startup items.

- **Accounts:** collects settings for the accounts that connect to your PC locally.
  - **Your info:** displays the account information.
  - **Email & accounts:** you can associate email addresses and business/school accounts with your computer.

- **Sign-in options:** allows you to configure new access modes such as Windows Hello (unlock with your face), graphic password and PIN. You can also change your password from here.
  - **Access work or school:** a panel for linking to a business account.
  - **Family:** lets you add people and form a family group with varying permissions by linking a Microsoft account, you can form a familiar user group with different permissions.
- **Time & Language:** corresponds to the old International Settings where you could set date, time, and location parameters such as currency.
  - **Date & Time:** allows you to set the time zone, daylight saving time and synchronization server.
  - **Language & Region:** is a completely new feature for Windows, finally it's possible to change language even after installation.
  - **Typing:** settings for the touch keyboard, autocorrection and other related settings.
  - **Speech:** Allows you to choose the language of speech recognition and voice for synthesis.
- **Gaming:** settings for the Game Bar, online streaming, and Xbox online.
  - **Game Bar:** check the game bar shortcuts.
  - **Game Mode:** optimize your PC for play by turning things off in the background.
  - **Captures:** settings for screenshot and games clip for gaming recordings.
- **Accessibility:** collects numerous parameters to enable accessibility features.
  - **Vision:** manages color enhancement, changing the appearance of the pointer to make it easier to see, magnifying glass and other features for people with visual impairments.
  - **Hearing:** group the audio volume settings and activation of Mono output, parameters for displaying subtitles.

- **Interaction:** brings together tools for interacting with virtual keyboards and voice commands, including the new Optical Control, which is still in the experimental phase
- **Privacy:** a very important settings section that manages Windows and app permissions for the camera, contacts, calendar, emails, and more.
- **Privacy & Security:** you can manage all settings for the Windows Security permissions
- **Windows Update::** gathers updates released by Microsoft. It is useful to check regularly if your PC is up to date, and if there is a slowdown, the updates might be the cause.

There are many items, but the important thing is getting oriented in this new interface. There will be many tutorials available and if you have a PC or virtual machine where the consequences are not serious, I recommend experimenting with the new settings.

You can open the Settings panel by pressing the Windows + I buttons simultaneously.

Notification Center

Compared to Windows 10, Microsoft has given a different organization to the notification center that appears renewed and organized in a different way. It contains all the notifications issued by the PC applications. It's not just "you got a message from..." or "Wake up!" or "Reminder for 23:34!" but also the old notification from programs in the taskbar.

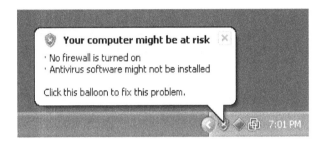

If you've missed a message from your antivirus or video card drivers: do not worry. It will all be collected as in your smartphone!

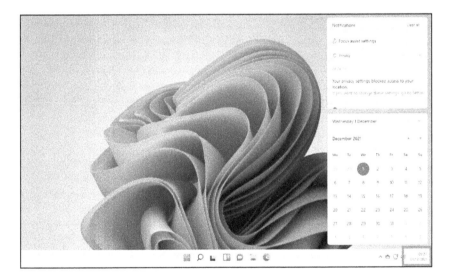

Quick Settings panel

Compared to Windows 10 where the quick settings were contained in the notification center, Windows 11 has a new section entirely dedicated to them.

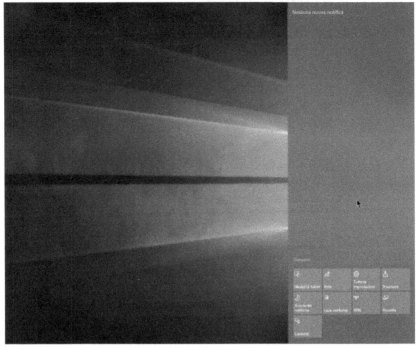

25 The Windows 10 notification area included notifications and quick settings within the same screen.

To access it, simply click on the area at the bottom right next to the system date and time.

Inside you can activate and deactivate various system parameters such as:

- **Airplane mode:** disable wireless connections, including Wi-Fi, Bluetooth, data connection.
- **Wi-Fi:** enables you to turn your Wi-Fi connection on or off and select the network to connect to.
- **Bluetooth:** allows you to turn on or off and manage connected devices.
- **Brightness**: adjust the screen brightness.
- **Volume:** controls the speaker volume.

- **Energy Saving:** activates or deactivates the energy saving mode to increase battery life and/or reduce energy consumption.
- **Accessibility:** enables various accessibility settings for disabled people such as magnifying glass, color filters, mono audio, real-time subtitles.

These quick settings may vary depending on your PC configuration. If, for example, you have a desktop computer without wireless networks and Bluetooth connection the switches will not be shown.

Where is Cortana?

With the arrival of Windows 11, Microsoft has introduced a major change in how users interact with the operating system. In fact, Cortana is no longer active. On some older online guides, it is often recommended to search for it in the Search box at the bottom of the taskbar but, however, once started the only thing it does is show an error screen.

Copilot: based on Artificial Intelligence

What will have replaced our virtual assistant? Of course, with artificial intelligence! I introduce you to Copilot. This evolution represents a significant step forward, combining the versatility of a voice and text interface with the power of an AI (=Artificial Intelligence). Copilot integrates deeply into Windows 11 to provide full, customized support.

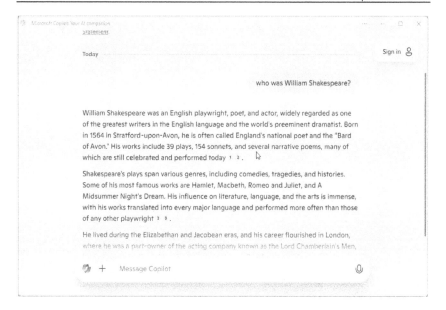

How does Copilot work?

The Copilot engine is powered by a custom version of GPT-4, one of the most advanced artificial intelligence models developed by Microsoft. This model is based on a large neural network, trained on a wide range of textual data to understand and generate natural language.

In fact, just as a child would do, artificial intelligence studies the world around it to provide answers in natural, user-friendly language and, above all, possess a wide knowledge base to give adequate responses

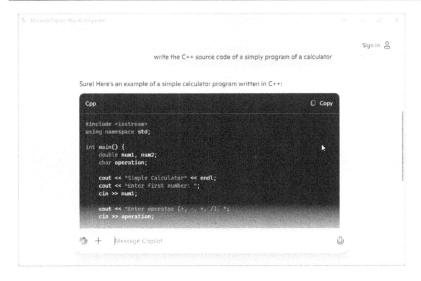

How to use Copilot on Windows 11

Copilot is accessible via web browser, but has been integrated into Windows 11 with update 24H2 (2024 Update). This version introduced several changes to the integration of Copilot, converting it into a web application that can be added to the taskbar.

Built-in Applications

Built-in Applications

Windows 11, like its predecessors Windows 10, Windows 8.1 and Windows 8, has two distinct categories of programs:

- **Desktop app:** traditional software for Windows;
- **Universal Apps:** universal applications for Windows 11 and Windows Phone, more mobile-oriented than PC.

Desktop applications can be found online or on common media. Universal Apps are available from the Windows Store. Just like in iOS and Android, there is an app that acts as an online store where there are different products, both free and paid.

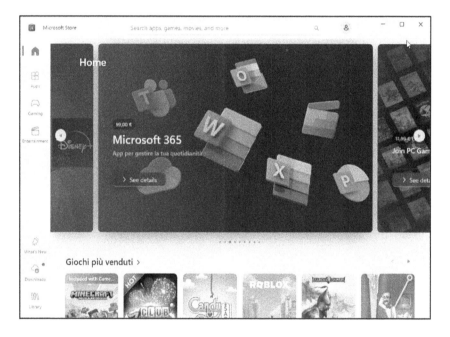

Many are already included in the operating system, such as:

- **Calculator.**
- **Microsoft Edge:** Windows 11 default browser (application for internet browsing).
- **Calendar:** app for marking appointments.
- **Movies and TV:** Virtual video library dedicated to films and TV series.
- **Photos:** a photo gallery of the PC. It also includes photo editing and photo enhancement tools.

- **Camera:** a simple app for taking photos using your PC's webcam or your tablet/convertible PC's camera.
- **Weather:** weather and temperature information.
- **Microsoft Outlook:** the replacement of the old Outlook Express, now available in a more spartan version and suitable for tablet use;
- **Microsoft Teams:** an app for communication and collaboration, ideal for meetings and video calls.
- **OneDrive:** cloud storage service to access and sync files from any device. Free up to 5GB of space occupied.

Alternative browsers

In 1998 the antitrust case against Microsoft brought the Redmond company to trial for holding an illegal monopoly in the web browser market, mainly through the inclusion of Internet Explorer in the Windows operating system. In fact, providing an already integrated application made it easy for the user to use what they found. In 2001 Microsoft changed some company policies and since then began the culture of choosing your favorite browser.

There are several alternative browsers to Microsoft Edge, which I remind you is preinstalled within Windows 11:

- **Google Chrome:** currently the most widely used in the world and with the largest number of plugins;
- **Mozilla Firefox:** open-source application with a focus on privacy and customization;
- **Opera:** a browser that offers built-in ad blockers and a free VPN.

These are some of the most popular and available to the average user. However, there are many others on the net.

Microsoft Edge

How to delete browsing data

Browsing data (history of websites visited, cookies, download history, etc.) can also be deleted in Microsoft Edge. You can do this either manually or when you close your browser.

1. Open Microsoft Edge.
2. Go to the main menu ⋯ at the top right.

3. From the menu click on the **Settings** item.
4. Open the **Privacy, search and services** section (you can find it by clicking on the icon ☰ in the upper left).
5. Click on **Clear Browsing Data.**
6. Click on **Choose what to clear.**
7. Select the time interval from the drop-down menu ("Last hour", "Last 24 hours", "Last 7 Days", "Last 4 Weeks", "All Time").
8. Select the types of data to delete (for example, "Browsing History", "Download History", "Cookies and other site data").

9. Click on **Clear Now** to delete.

Enable deletion at every close

1. Repeat steps 1-5 from the previous paragraph.
2. Click on Choose what to clear every time you close the browser.

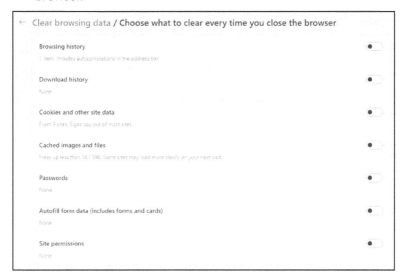

3. On the screen you can select which elements to delete when you close your browser, from history to stored passwords.

Developer Tools

For web developers, every browser has the functionality to examine the HTML and CSS code of web pages. Microsoft Edge also has these two items in the browser context menu (right-click on the open page), however you need to enable them.

1. Open Microsoft Edge.
2. Press **F12** on your keyboard.
3. Click on **Open DevTools** to enable development tools.

To use them you will need only to:

1. Right click on any element of the web page.
2. Press F12 or click on **Inspect** to view both element inspection and source code.

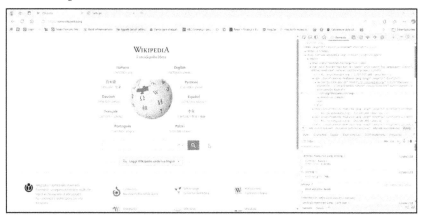

Plugins for Edge

Microsoft Edge, as well as other browsers, allows you to install different extensions. Some are directly provided by the manufacturer, such as Office Online, others have been published on the *Windows Store*.

1. Open Microsoft Edge.
2. Go to the main menu ⋯ at the top right.
3. Click on the Extensions menu item.

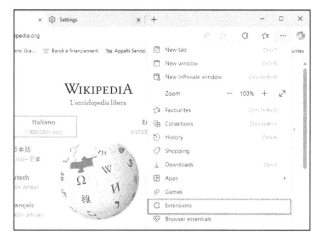

4. To enter the store and find new extensions click on the button Get Extensions for Microsoft Edge.
5. A rich screen will open with extensions for the most disparate functions: from ad block to VPNs, etc. You'll just have to choose one and click on Install;
6. Read the permissions required by the extension and click on Add Extension. The browser will download and install the extension automatically.

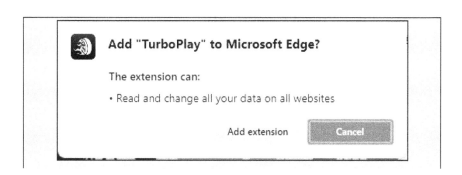

Microsoft Edge informs you of the actions an extension can take within your browser. For example, the Adblocker shown in the screenshot will prevent ads from appearing on the web pages you visit, but to do so, it needs to read and modify the pages and change your privacy settings in order to work. For this reason, be sure to check what you install. Rely on extensions reviewed by users and reliable sources.

How to change your default search engine

If you are also used to using Google as a search engine instead of Microsoft Bing but don't want to stop using Edge, you can change it.

1. Open the main menu ⋯ at the top right.
2. Click on **Settings** from the contextual menu.
3. Open the **Privacy, search and services** section (you can find it by clicking on the icon ☰ in the upper left).
4. Click on **Search and connected experiences**.
5. Click on **Address Bar and search**.

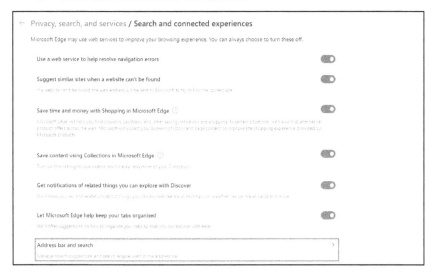

6. Select a search engine from the drop-down menu in the Search engine used in the address bar section.

Change default Downloads folder

Microsoft Edge saves all downloaded files to the Downloads folder in your personal directory. **This is only done if at the time the browser asks what to do you click on Save and not on Save As.**

1. Open the main menu ⋯ at the top right.
2. Click on **Settings** from the contextual menu.
3. Open the **Downloads** section (you can find it by clicking on the icon ☰ in the upper left).
4. Click on **Change**.
5. Select the new folder to save downloads in, then click on **Select Folder**.

Set the file path request for each download

Edge can ask each download where to save it and also give an actual confirmation that you want to download the files. To do this, enable Ask me what to do with each download in the screen above.

How to manage the stored passwords

Microsoft Edge has an archive of saved passwords, where you can manage them and, by entering the PC password, consult their content.

1. Click the three-dot icon (menu) in the top right corner.
2. Select **Settings** from the drop-down menu.
3. Scroll down to the **Wallet** section and click **Password**.
4. On this screen you can manage saved passwords or add new ones. You can also import and export a password archive.

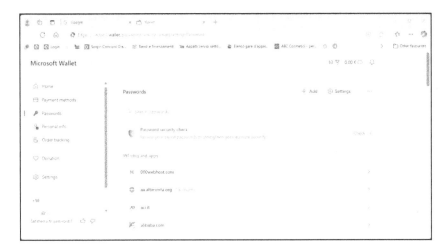

To consult a saved password, simply click the site it's associated with, enter your PC's password and click on the eye icon to view it.

How to delete all the stored passwords

Microsoft Edge stores all saved passwords. However, you may need to prevent the browser from retaining your previously stored credentials.

1. Click on the three-dot icon (menu) in the top right of the window;
2. Select **Settings** from the drop-down menu;

3. Click on **Privacy, search and services** on the left (you can find it by clicking on the icon ≡ in the upper left corner);

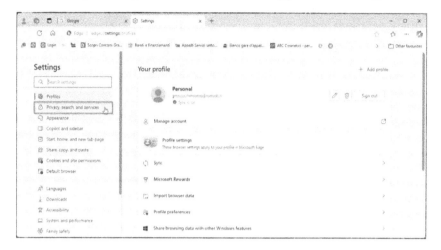

4. Go to the section **Delete Browsing Data;**
5. Click on **Choose what to clear.**
6. Select as time interval **All Time;**
7. Deselect all boxes and select only **Passwords;**
8. Click on **Clear now.**

Notepad

The Notepad in Windows 11 has been greatly enriched with features. For those who do not know it, it is a simple text editor (without formatting: that is, it only allows you to write text without colors, fonts, sizes and layout of any kind). It is perfect for quickly taking notes and, above all, for editing source codes, system files, etc.

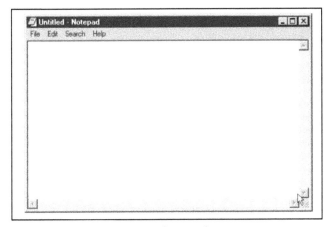

90s Notepad Screenshot.

Generally, the look of the Notepad has been the same over the years, but in Windows 11 it has undergone an evolution.

Prevent Tabs from Opening in Notepad

What stands immediately out are the tabs: it is now possible to open multiple text documents within the same window. One potentially annoying aspect is that tabs will automatically reopen even when Notepad is restarted. This feature can be turned off.

1. Open Notepad;
2. Click on Settings (gear icon in the top right corner).

3. Scroll down to the Notepad Opening section

4. Click on When Notepad starts.
5. Activate Start new session and discard unsaved changes.

As indicated in the settings, instead of saving everything automatically when the application closes, Notepad will delete unsaved files. Of course, it will prompt you to decide whether or not you wish to save the changes.

Change the font size

To resize the text inside Notepad, you can:

1. Press the combination **CTRL + +** to enlarge the text and **CTRL + -** to make it smaller. Press **CTRL + 0** to bring everything back to the default value.
2. Alternatively, click on the **View** menu and, within the **Zoom** entry, click on the respective options for magnifying, reducing or resetting to the default value.

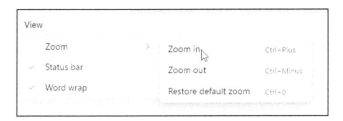

How to change default font and its size

Since it's a simple text editor, the font is a monospace at 11 pt. A monospaced font (or fixed-width) ensures that each character occupies the same horizontal space, regardless of width. It is generally used by developers to improve the readability of code.

Ciao   Ciao
Ciao   Ciao

You can change the font of Notepad:

1. Open Notepad.
2. Click on the settings (gear icon in the top right).
3. In the **Font** section, choose the font family (that is, the name of the font), the style (if regular, light, bold and then the weight of the font) and the size.

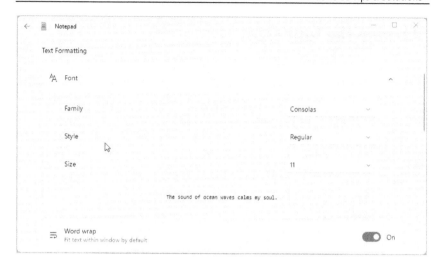

Notepad keyboard shortcuts

Keyboard Shortcuts	Actions
Ctrl + N	New file
Ctrl + O	Open file
Ctrl + S	Save file
Ctrl + Shift + S	Save As
Ctrl + P	Print
Ctrl + Z	Undo the previous action
Ctrl + Y	Redo the cancelled action
Ctrl + A	Select all the text
Ctrl + C	Copy the selected text
Ctrl + X	Cut the selected text
Ctrl + V	Paste the copied or cut text
Ctrl + F	Find
Ctrl + H	Find and Replace
Ctrl + Shift + N	New window
Ctrl + Shift + E	Opens the "Explore" window
Ctrl + W	Close a tab or window with a single Notepad tab

Calculator

The Windows 11 calculator has been improved in terms of design and functionality. You can resize it to different shapes and sizes.

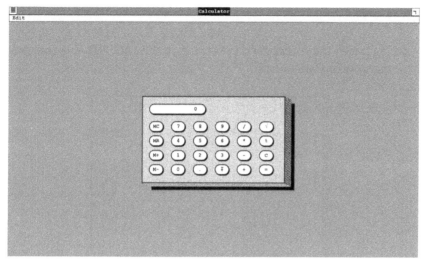

26 Windows 1.0 Calculator (1985)

It can be used in four ways:
- **Standard:** simple calculator with basic arithmetic functions.
- **Scientific:** includes advanced calculation functions such as trigonometric (sine, cosine, tangent) and other mathematical operations.
- **Graphing:** provides a graphical representation of the mathematical expressions entered.
- **Programmer:** designed for programmers, it supports binary, octal and hexadecimal calculations, bitwise operations and other specific functions.
- **Date Calculation:** the calculator includes useful functions for calculating dates, such as counting days between two dates and adding or subtracting years, months or days to a date.
- **Converter:** allows you to convert units of measurement such as volume, length, weight, temperature, energy and more.

Keep the calculator in the foreground

This very useful feature allows you to keep your calculator in the foreground. In fact, having to reopen the calculator while you are consulting a document and having it close repeatedly can be frustrating!

To keep it in the foreground you can press the ALT + UP Arrow or click on the appropriate button.

Show history of operations

Just like desktop calculators there is a paper tape with the history of operations performed, also the software version includes a digital version of this function.

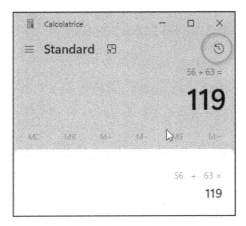

Keyboard shortcuts

Here are some keyboard shortcuts to use the calculator without taking your hands off the keyboard.

Keyboard Shortcuts	Action
ESC	Clears the current input
Backspace	Delete the last digit entered
Enter	Performs the calculation
Alt + 1	Standard mode
Alt + 2	Scientific mode
Alt + 3	Graphing Mode
Alt + 4	Programming mode
Alt + 5	Date calculation mode
Ctrl + H	Show the history
Ctrl + M	Stores the current number
Ctrl + P	Adds the current number to memory
Ctrl + Q	Subtracts the current number from memory
CTRL + R	Recall the stored number
Ctrl + L	Clear memory
+	Add
-	Subtract
*	Multiply
/	Divide

Difference between two dates

1. Open Date Calculation mode (you can find it in the menu on the left ☰).
2. Enter the dates.
3. The calculator will give you the difference.

Add or subtract days

1. Open the Date Calculation mode (you can find it in the menu on the left ☰).
2. Enter the starting date.
3. Choose whether to add or subtract.
4. Set the time interval in years, months, and days.

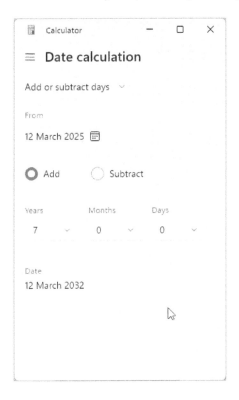

Currency

1. Open the Currency mode (you can find it in the menu on the left ☰).

2. Select the currency to start from and enter the amount and currency in which to convert.

3. To stay up-to-date with exchange values click on **Update rates**.

Microsoft Outlook

In 2024, the new Outlook was launched on Windows 11. It offers a more modern and integrated email and calendar management experience.

Opening the Outlook icon will open the new application. If you don't have a configured Microsoft account, you may need to set up a new account from scratch.

> Do not confuse it with Microsoft Office Outlook. Just like in the '90s and 2000s there was Outlook Express, a limited version of Microsoft Office Outlook, today there is the basic Outlook. However, the application in the Office suite is much more advanced and is generally the most used professionally.

Which providers does Outlook support?

Outlook allows you to enter Microsoft, Gmail, Yahoo! , iCloud and all services that connect via IMAP, as well as compatible business and school accounts.

By entering your username and following the login process you can link your mail accounts. For IMAP email providers or corporate accounts the process may require additional steps.

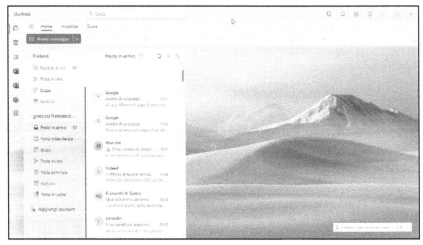

27 The new Windows 11 Outlook.

As reported by several users on the network, this application is essentialy the Outlook web installed within the operating system.

How to write a new mail

1. Click on top left New Mail;
2. Use the commands described on the next page;
3. Once you have finished composing the email click on Send.

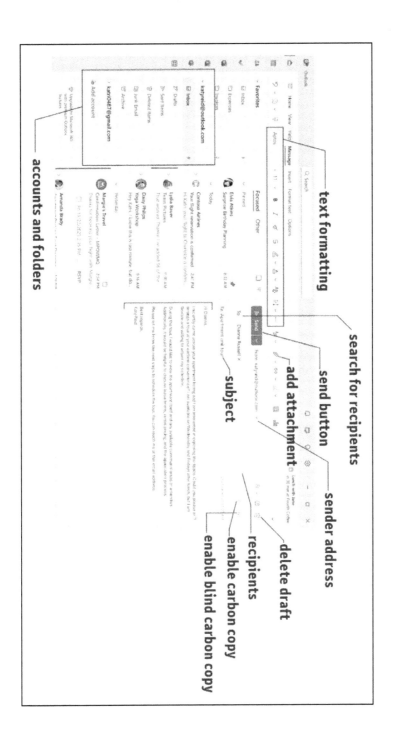

text formatting

search for recipients

send button

sender address

add attachment

delete draft

recipients

enable carbon copy

enable blind carbon copy

subject

accounts and folders

Set up a signature for your emails

1. Write a new message.
2. Click on the signature icon in the formatting bar..

3. Enter a name for the signature and write its content.
4. Once you have completed the signature, click on the **Save** button;
5. To add another one, click on **New Signature**;
6. In the **Select default signatures** section, you can select which of the signatures to use by default for both new messages and replies and forwards.

Clock

The Windows 11 Clock App includes several useful features for managing your time.

- **Focus sessions**: this new version of Windows lets you to define work or study sessions in which you can deactivate notifications to increase your concentration.

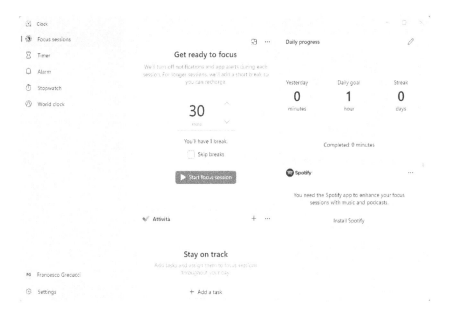

You can start a focus session by clicking on date and time in the bottom right of the taskbar. Just click on the **Focus** button.

- **Timer:** define one or more timers.
- **Alarm Clock:** set one or more alarms.
- **Stopwatch:** a stopwatch on your PC.
- **International Clock:** shows time from different parts of the world.

Paint

Microsoft Paint has been one of the symbols of Windows since its first version in 1985, named PAINTBRUSH for Windows 1.0.

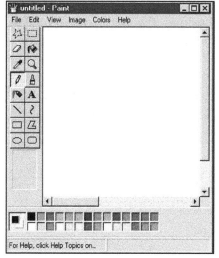

28 The iconic Paint screen. Windows 95 (1995)

It has remained almost unchanged over time, but with Windows 11, significant changes have been made, including:

- A more modern interface with several more advanced drawing features suitable for the use of a drawing pen.
- Management of levels to coordinate the different elements of a work separately.
- **Paint Co-creator:** a feature that uses artificial intelligence to create images from text prompts.

From the simplest drawing program on PC to a complete app for creating digital art with the help of AI!

Microsoft To Do

Microsoft To Do is designed to help you organize your days, set up reminders, and stay on top of your tasks. Here are some of the main features of Microsoft To Do:

- **Task lists divided into categories** – Create custom lists to organize your activities based on different projects or themes.
- **Reminders for important deadlines** – Set due dates and get notifications to ensure you never miss an important task.
- **Prioritization** – Organize your tasks by priority and highlight the most urgent ones to stay on top of your work.
- **Integration with Microsoft 365** – Sync your tasks seamlessly with Outlook and OneNote for a more connected workflow.
- **Access from any device** – Your tasks are always with you! Access them from your PC, smartphone, tablet, or other computers.
- **Collaboration** – Share your lists with friends, family, or colleagues to work together efficiently.

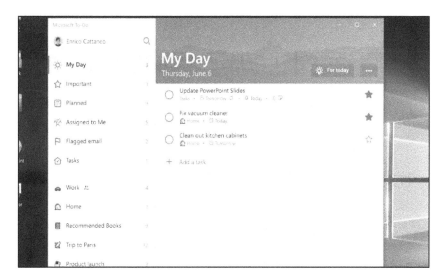

Windows Security

Windows Security is the control center for Windows security. It includes built-in antivirus settings, Microsoft account protection, firewall parameters, unrecognized files check in apps and browsers, hardware protection for virtual machines, the improvement of system performance and Parental Control to protect children's activity.

To access it, just open the *Settings* and go to Privacy & Security > Windows Security.

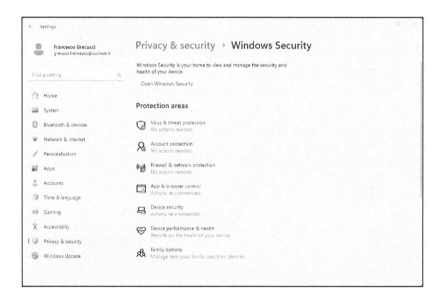

Solitaire & Casual Games

Among the applications integrated in Windows 11, one cannot miss the historical solitaire. Its name is Microsoft Solitaire Collection and it offers a selection of solitaires, including the classic Windows solitaire: Klondike.

Automate Repetitive Tasks with Power Automate

Power Automate is a Microsoft application that allows users to create automated workflows between their favorite apps and services to sync files, get notifications, collect data and more. For example, you can create an automation that sends you an email based on a certain action performed on your PC. Power Automate is a real programming language that uses a visual interface, allowing users to build small programs using predefined blocks. This allows to create automation flows even without having special programming skills.

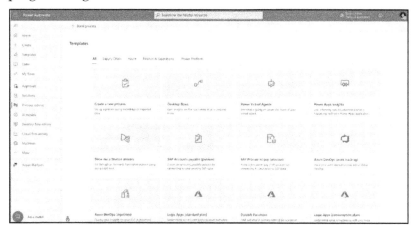

Power Automate is the Microsoft equivalent of iOS **Shortcuts** and Mac **Automator**. The operation is very similar and allows you to automate repetitive operations based on predetermined inputs.

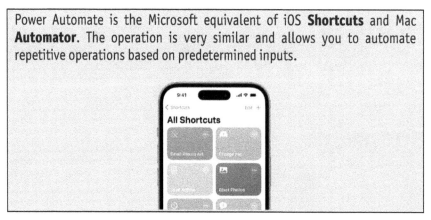

User Guides

User Guides

How to check which version of Windows is installed

Which version of Windows 11 do I have? There may be significant changes between versions, both in terms of functionality and compatibility with applications. Even if you have Windows 11 installed, you might need to update it if your version is no longer supported to avoid security risks.

1. Open the Power User Menu (**Windows + X** key combination or right-click on the start button)
2. Click on **System**
3. Check the version in the **Version** field.

How to install and manage apps through the Microsoft Store

Windows 11 has enhanced the Microsoft Store with a faster and smoother experience. To download an app, just:

1. Open the **Microsoft Store** by clicking on the 🔳 in the taskbar or by searching for it in the search box.
2. Search for the application you want to download or browse categories.
3. Open the page of the application you are interested in and click on **Get**. The application will be installed like any other program in Windows.

How to enable Night Light

Screens emit light that affects sleep quality and vision, potentially causing issues like insomnia and retinal disorders. Night mode, enabled by software, shifts colors to warmer tones by reducing blue light brightness, a color that can create the disturbances mentioned above. In a nutshell, the screen looks slightly yellowed but you feel less visual effort, which can help you sleep better after work. The night mode is automatically activated at scheduled times, usually from 9:00 PM to 7:00 AM, or by setting a location based on sunrise and sunset.

1. Open Settings.
2. Go to **System** > Display
3. Enable the **Night Light** switch. It will be activated automatically at 9:00 PM and deactivated automatically at 7:00 AM the following day.
4. To change the schedule time or night color temperature, click on Schedule night light.

Quick activation

To quickly activate the night light, simply open Quick Settings (bottom right on the taskbar) and click on Night Light.

How to manage disk space usage

In Windows 11 Settings, under the **System > Storage** section, you can view the disk space usage occupied in an organized manner.

By clicking on **Show more categories,** the system divides the various file and folder categories that occupy storage space, allowing you to take action where necessary to free up space. This way, you can identify the largest folders or files and decide whether to delete them or move them to an external drive. With this feature, you can keep your device efficient and free of unnecessary files.

How to use Snap Layouts

Snap Layouts is the new feature in Windows 11 that allows you to organize open windows into various configurations on your screen. This makes multitasking more efficient and you can use multiple apps at the same time neatly, easily, and quickly.

1. Open the application you want to organize.
2. **Hover** over the window's zoom button (top right).

3. Select one of the layouts you want to use. The layouts with icons of other applications allow you to move the currently open apps according to the diagram shown.

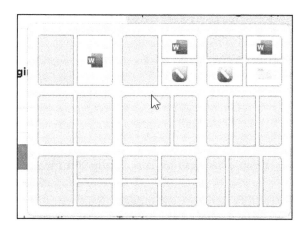

4. If your layout has empty slots, the system will ask which of the open apps you want to use.

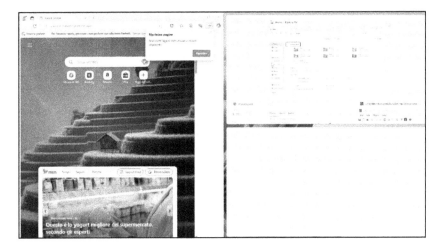

Snap Layouts can also be used by dragging a window to the bar that appears at the top and defining the layout as in the previous example.

How can I disable Snap Layouts?

If Snap Layouts is not to your liking you can disable it so that you no longer have the various elements that appear when you move the windows or click on the zoom icon. To do this:

1. Open Settings.
2. Click on **System** on the left.
3. Click on **Multi-tasking**.
4. Deactivate the option **Snap Windows**.

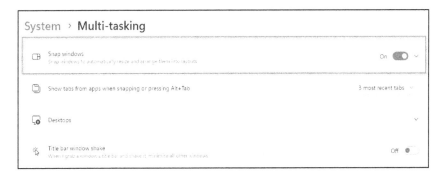

How to align two windows in side-by-side columns

Do you have one window with a PDF open and another with Microsoft Word ready to make a summary for your studies? Are you tired of having to close and reopen two screens? Do you think it would be useful to buy another screen? **Or simply…you can put them next to each other!**

1. Open the window you want to see on the left side and press the Windows + Left Arrow;
2. Choose the window you want to see on the right side from the options and click on its preview.

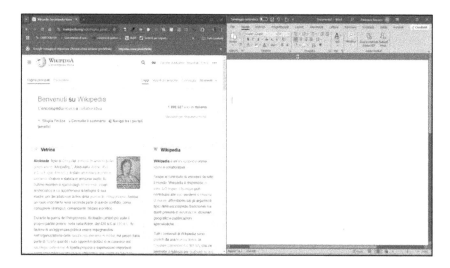

How to disconnect a user

Users can be disconnected. This means that everything open inside it is terminated and the account is disconnected, a bit like when the PC is turned off, but without actually turning it off.

1. Open the Start Menu.
2. Click on your user icon.
3. Click on **Sign Out.**

On some versions of Windows 11 the process may vary slightly.

1. Open the Start Menu.
2. Click on your user icon.
3. Click on **Sign Out.**

How to temporarily lock the computer with a password

Windows has the possibility, with a keyboard shortcut, to lock the computer and display the login screen, without disconnecting the user session. It is essential to have a password set also for the access to Windows, otherwise the lock will easily bypassed by the Login button.

1. Press the **Windows + L** keyboard shortcut.
2. Insert your password or PIN or your default login method to unlock your PC.

How to set (or change) your user password

1. Go to Settings.
2. On the left sidebar, click on Account.
3. Click on Sign-in options.

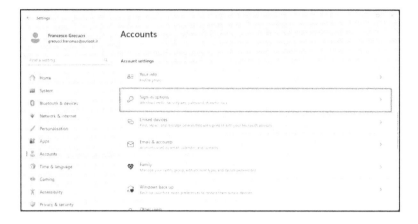

4. Under the Password section click on the Add (or Change) button.

Change other sign-in options

With the procedure described above, you can also add or change the other sign-in options included in Windows 11. There are also:
- **Facial Recognition:** you can access your PC with your face.
- **Fingerprint recognition:** you can log in using your finger.
- **PIN:** you can sign in with a PIN.
- **Security Key:** you can log in by using a physical security key.

Of course, except the PIN option, your PC must be compatible with the various options.

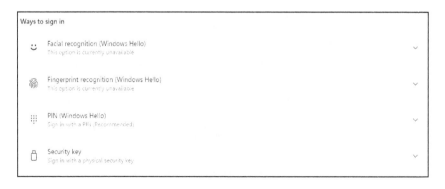

How to set a profile image

Want to give your PC a personal touch with a profile picture? Here's how to set a profile image for your account.

1. Open Settings.
2. On the left click on **Accounts**.
3. Click on **Your Info**.

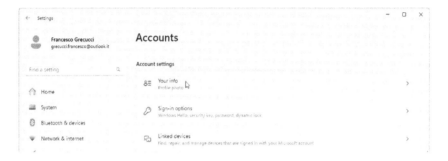

1. You can take a photo of yourself directly from the webcam by clicking on **Open Camera** or choose a file from your PC by clicking on **Browse Files**.

How to create a new user

Windows allows multiple users to log in with different passwords and have their own desktop and data separately, even their own applications if you choose to install them only for the logged-in user. To create a new user:

1. Open Settings.
2. On the left, click on Accounts.
3. Scroll down to Other users.

4. Click on Add account.
5. Choose the type of account to add:
   a. If you want to add a Microsoft Account (linked to the Microsoft online service), enter your email and password.
   b. If you prefer to add a traditional account, click I don't have this person's sign-in information and Add a user without a Microsoft account.

6. If you have chosen to add a traditional account, please enter your username and password as well as the security questions.

7. Sign out of your account.
8. After completing the setup, you will find your new account on the login screen.

How to customize your PC with Themes

Those who have been using Windows for several years will remember that from Windows 95 with Microsoft Plus onwards, MS offered different styles of user interface customization called Themes. Themes are just a collection of color styles, text, background images and other effects to give your PC a different touch!

29 One of the first PC themes in 1995 came with Microsoft Plus! Back then, the package wasn't free; in fact, it was a full-fledged software product that had to be purchased, complete with a box.

1. Right-click on an empty area of the desktop.
2. Click on the Personalise menu item.

3. Inside the Personalisation screen you will find a set of default themes.
4. Click on one of them to change your system's skin.

You can customize your theme even more by clicking on **Themes**. Inside the themes section you can edit the background (both images and solid colors), the colors of the user interface, the sound scheme and the mouse pointer style.

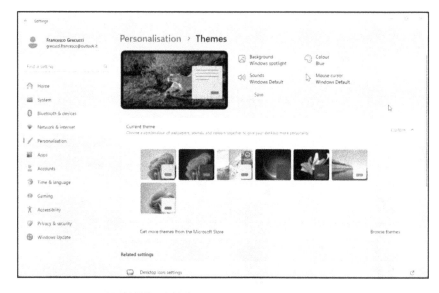

By clicking on **Browse Themes** you can download or buy others from the Microsoft Store.

How to customize the Start menu

The start menu in Windows 11 can be customized to your own preferences for use and display. To enter the customization of the start menu:

1. Open Settings.
2. On the left click on **Personalisation**.
3. Click on **Start**.

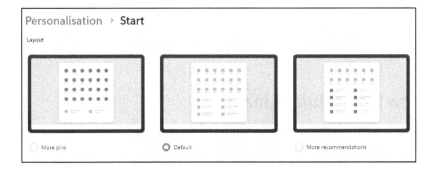

The first setting is that of the layout:
1. **More pins:** it gives more space to the favorite apps and less to the recommended elements.
2. **Default:** is the standard view divided between app and recommended items.
3. **More reccomendations:** gives more space to the recommended items and less to the apps.

The other settings allow you to choose whether to show recently added apps, the most used ones, decide whether to show recommended and recent files (usually the documents that you open most often and those opened recently).

How to set Quick Links

In the Start Settings you can define quick links. They're right next to the power off button.

You can set them by clicking on Folders in the Start settings.

How to disable app advertisement in the Start menu

Windows 11 may display promotional information for some apps. These are tips for buying or even simply downloading free apps from a curated group of developers to help you discover some of the best apps available in the Microsoft store.

Since these ads tend to get confused with the applications installed on your PC, they could be misleading and annoying. To deactivate this type of advertising:

1. Open the Settings app.
2. On the left, select Personalisation.
3. Find the Start section and click on It.
4. Turn off the Show recommendations for tips, shortcuts, new apps, and more option.

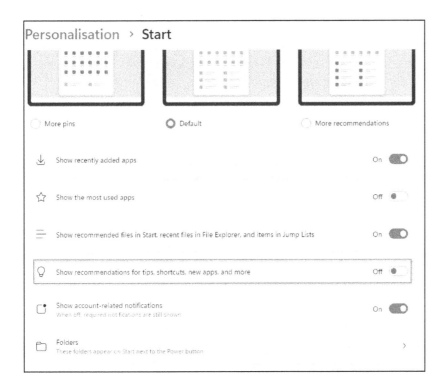

How to customize the lock screen

Always in the **customization** section of the settings, which I remember being reachable with the right button on the desktop or in **Settings > Personalisation** you can also customize the *Lock Screen*. This is the first screen you see when logging on to your computer or requesting a password after blocking a user.

30 Windows 11 Lock Screen

Customization involves setting the background image of the lock screen. You can entrust Windows to find a random image, set a static image of our preference or create an image presentation.

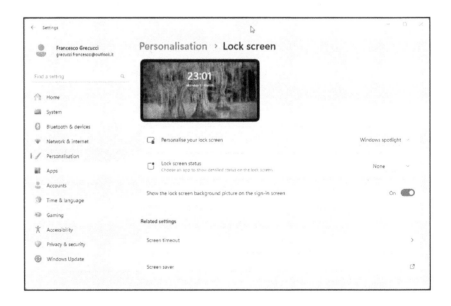

How to set a screensaver

The screensaver is a feature found in all operating systems with a graphical interface, which causes the screen to darken or display a series of images, animations, or videos after a set period of inactivity with the mouse or keyboard. In simple terms, it activates when there is no interaction between the user and the PC.

Two CRT screens.
unicron1bot, CC BY 2.0 <https://creativecommons.org/licenses/by/2.0>, via Wikimedia Commons

Originally, screensavers were used as a protective measure for CRT screens used as computer monitors. The risk of permanently burning certain areas of the screen due to displaying the same image for too long was high, leading to the so-called **screen burn-in (or ghost effect)**. You can observe this effect on monitors used for surveillance systems or informational displays, such as those in stations and airports. It appears as a sort of visible outline or shadow on the screen.

With the advent of LCD and LED monitors, this issue occurs much less frequently, and the screensaver has been replaced by a simple screen standby mode. However, you can still activate the screensaver for aesthetic reasons.

1. Open the Settings.
2. On the left click on Personalisation.
3. Click on Lock Screen.
4. Click on Screen saver.

5. Select one of the screensavers present in the system and click on Test to do a test.
6. In the Wait field you can define the idle minutes that will have to pass to activate the screen saver.
7. If you want the screensaver to block the user in such a way that any malicious actors cannot access your computer by leaving the screen saver, check the box On resume, display log-on screen.

8. To exit the screensaver you just need to move the mouse.

How to set the screen and computer standby timer

As I said in the previous guide, nowadays it is the screen to go into standby after a certain time of inactivity. But how do I define how many minutes must pass before the screen goes black?

1. Open the Settings.
2. On the left bar, click on **Personalisation**.
3. Click on **Lock Screen**.
4. Click on **Screen timeout**.
5. Click on **Screen and Sleep time-outs**.

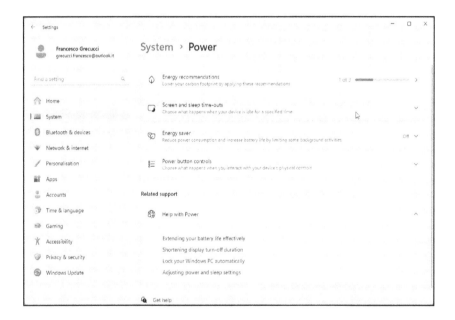

6. Define the idle time required to turn off the screen in the Turn my screen off after section This is divided into two modes (if using a laptop): when running on battery power or when connected to a power supply.

In this screen you can also set the computer's idle time before going into **sleep mode**.

How to disable stand-by

Windows 11 goes into standby after 30 minutes of inactivity. This setting can, however, be changed.

1. Right-click on the Menu Start.
2. Click on **Power Options**.
3. Click on **Screen and sleep time-outs**.
4. Select Never from the drop-down menu in the **Make my device sleep after** section.

How to increase system font size

In some situations, you may need to see what appears on the screen more clearly, with larger text. A common phrase from those who buy a high-resolution monitor is, *"Oh my, do I have to see everything this small?"* Very often, people make the mistake of lowering the resolution, resulting in a loss of quality that often only makes things worse. The elements on the screen will appear larger, sure, but the quality will be significantly degraded. **To solve this problem, you simply need to resize the text on the screen.** This applies not only to text but also to all on-screen components, such as icons, buttons, text boxes, etc.

1. Right click on an empty area of the desktop and click on **Display Settings**.

2. Under the **Scaling** section, select the checkbox indicating the percentage for text size. You can choose from the following levels: 100% (normal), 125%, 150%, and 175%. I recommend selecting **125%** to prevent on-screen elements from becoming too large and significantly reducing your workspace.

3. In order to apply the changes correctly, it may be necessary to disconnect the user or restart the PC.

Customised Scaling

By clicking on **Scaling**, you can access the **custom scaling** settings and choose the most suitable percentage yourself.

However, the predefined percentages are compatible with most applications. Using a non-standard scaling percentage may cause issues with the system and applications. In fact, this procedure is also discouraged by **Windows 11** itself.

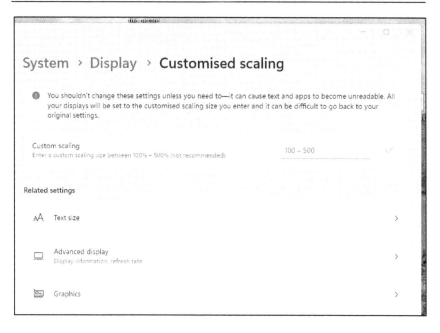

System › Display › **Customised scaling**

You shouldn't change these settings unless you need to—it can cause text and apps to become unreadable. All your displays will be set to the customised scaling size you enter and it can be difficult to go back to your original settings.

Custom scaling
Enter a custom scaling size between 100% – 500% (not recommended)

100 – 500

Related settings

A͞A   Text size   ›

▭   Advanced display
      Display information, refresh rate   ›

▦   Graphics   ›

How to change the system language

Finally, Microsoft has realized the importance of making their operating systems multilingual. Once upon a time, each installation CD contained only the default language of the country of sale, and finding a Language Pack was not easy. Today, it takes just a few clicks and an Internet connection to download different languages and use them as you need.

1. Open Settings.
2. On the left click on Time & Language.
3. Click on Language & region.
4. Inside Windows display language, usually only the one chosen during installation appears. Click on Add a language (or the + button and foreign language description) and type in the name of the language to install.

5. Click on the Next button (the blue icon, in case your PC is in an incomprehensible language that you need to change).

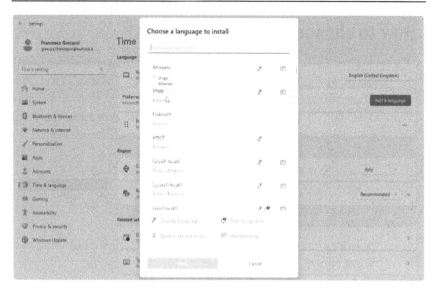

6. Select the language pack elements you want to install and click on **Install**.

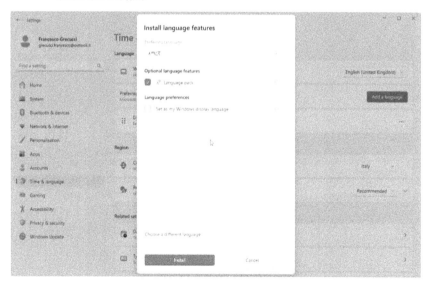

7. Once you have installed more languages will be available in the drop-down menu.
8. To apply the new settings, restart your PC.

How to change keyboard layout

PC keyboards are not all the same. The so-called layout determines the position of the keys depending on the input language, from the arrangement of the letters to the special characters. If your PC has a keyboard with a different layout than the software one, the keys will not correspond correctly and you may have difficulty typing.

1. Open Settings.
2. On the left, click on Time & Language.
3. Click on Language & Region.
4. Click on Add a language.
5. Choose the language you want and install it following the procedure.

6. Go back to the Language & Region screen.
7. Under the new language click on ... and then on Language options.

8. Inside the Language options go into the Keyboard section and click on Add a keyboard.

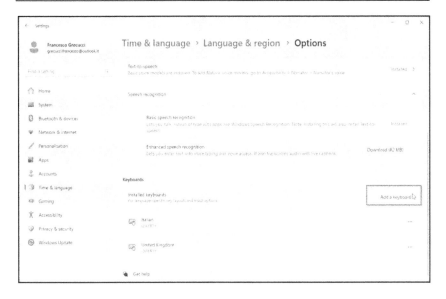

You can choose to have multiple keyboard layouts at the same time: to switch from one to another you just use the combination of Windows + Spacebar.

How to change timezone

Traveling with a small laptop is a good idea, but you have to be careful about time changes. If you don't have an internet connection your PC won't notice the change of location!

1. Right click on the time and date in the taskbar.
2. Click on **Adjust date and time**.

3. Uncheck **Set the time zone automatically**.
4. Enable Location Services if required.

5. Select the time zone of your location.

How to manually set date and time

If the PC cannot give a correct time, it may not be necessary to change only the time zone. To manually set the date and time, you must disable the option **Set the time automatically** and then, click on Change.

How to synchronize the time with Windows servers

It is possible, if you are connected to the internet, to synchronize the time with the Microsoft servers in Windows 11:

1. Open **Settings**.
2. On the left side, click on **Time and Language**.

3. Click **Date & Time.**
4. Under the **Additional settings** section click on Sync
    Now.

How to hide icons from desktop

If you want to enjoy the desktop background or the icons bother you, you can hide them without deleting them. The content will always be available in the Desktop folder within File Explorer when reactivated.

1. Right-click on an empty area of the desktop;
2. Click on Show more options;
3. Click on View;
4. Uncheck the Show desktop icons box.
5. All icons, including the Recycle Bin will disappears.

▶ How to make them reappear

1. Right-click on an empty area of the desktop;
2. Click on Show more options;
3. Click on View;
4. Check the Show desktop icons box.
5. All icons will reappear.

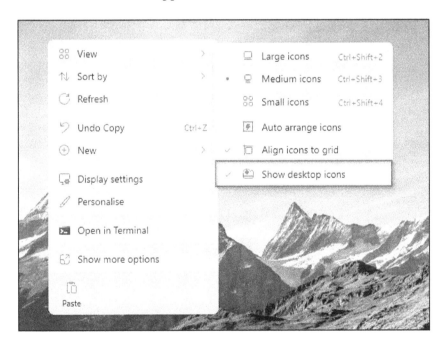

How to print/export to PDF

Windows 11 offers an extremely useful feature that has long been requested by its users: the possibility to export documents in PDF format. In fact, since Office 2007 this format has been available as an output option. However, having a built-in virtual printer built into the system makes things much easier by allowing all applications to export to PDF.

1. Any document you want to export to PDF, click on the Print window of the program you are working on;
   Select the Microsoft Print to PDF printer and click on Print.

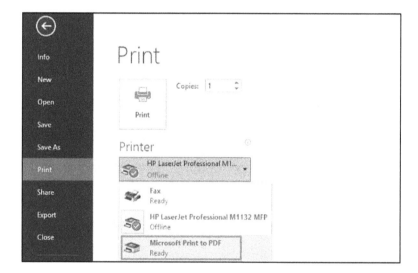

2. Choose where to save the file.

How to use Volume Mixer

The Volume Mixer in Windows allows you to adjust the volume of your speakers or headphones. You can increase and decrease both the overall volume and the individual applications. Use this window to mute or prioritize certain applications.

1. To open the Volume Mixer, right-click the audio icon in the bottom-right corner.

2. Click on **Open Volume Mixer**.

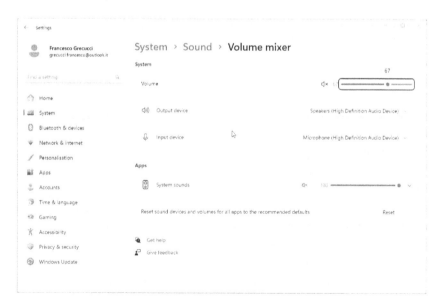

As you may have noticed, among the applications there is the **System Sounds** control. It's nothing more than the volume of sounds emitted by Windows. If you are listening to music at high volume, for example, you can turn it down or turn it off to avoid hearing warning or error sounds at a high volume.

How to set the mouse for left-handed use

Windows almost always adapts to the needs of its users. Among these, there is the possibility of using the mouse even for left-handed users. Simply move the mouse to the other side of the keyboard and reverse the buttons: the right will become the main button, while the left will be the secondary one.

1. Open Settings.
2. On the left, select Bluetooth and Devices.
3. Click on Mouse.
4. Select Right from the Primary mouse button box.

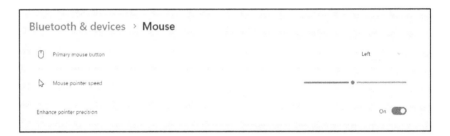

Caution: in many cases mice, especially the older ones, can be used with both hands. However, there are devices designed specifically for the right hand (for example, some Microsoft mice). You may want to consider buying a left-handed mouse, as prolonged use of a traditional mouse could be uncomfortable and even cause tendinitis.

How to enable mono audio

Music, film and video have been using stereophony for over 30 years. This technology allows the sound to be differentiated between the two speakers, ensuring that the original sound source is reproduced as faithfully as possible. In a movie, for example, if a car is speeding from one side of the screen to the other, the sound is also manipulated to create this illusion. However, there may be situations where you have to turn off stereo audio, making it necessary to switch to mono audio.

1.   Open Windows Settings.
2.   Click on Accessibility.
3.   Go to Audio under the Hearing tab.

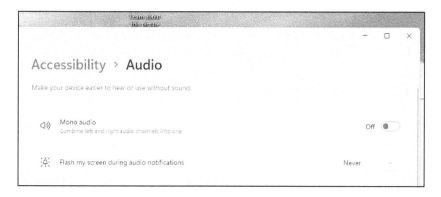

4.   Enable the Mono audio option.

How to group open applications

Inside the taskbar - near Search - there is a button like this: ▙. It allows you to group all the windows of the open applications. Just click on the application preview to enter it. You can also call this function with the key combination Windows + TAB.

Virtual Desktops

By clicking on New Desktop you can create one or more virtual desktops. It's an invention from a few years ago, introduced on Linux systems, where you can organize different applications across multiple virtual desktops. This means that if you're working in a Word and Excel environment at the same time, you can create a new one with Netflix to watch your favorite TV series. Just press the combination of keys Windows + CTRL + Arrow to switch between the various virtual environments. Simply put, pretend to work and come back to Netflix whenever you want. *Of course, wear the headphones, the audio does not go off when you switch to the other desktop...*

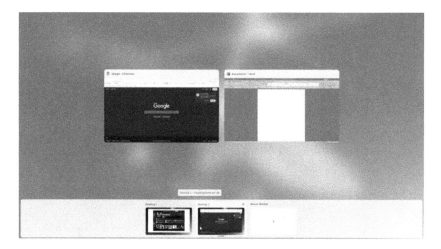

How to install a font

A font is nothing more than a writing style. Its characteristics and the original character design are stored in a file. For Windows, usually you download and install TrueType. These files, characterized by the .ttf extension, are widely available online either for free or for purchase.

1. Right click on the character file you downloaded.
2. Click on Install.
3. You will be able to use your new font from the list of fonts available in your word processing, graphics and editing programs.

How to create a compressed archive (ZIP, 7Z, TAR) directly in Windows

Windows 11 allows you to create compressed archives directly from the File Explorer. A compressed archive is a file that contains one or more files within it, reducing the overall size through data compression. This process saves disk space and makes files transfer easier.

1. Open File Explorer.
2. Navigate within the folder of files or folders you want to compress (you can hold down the Ctrl key to select multiple files).
3. Right-click on the selection and click Compress to...

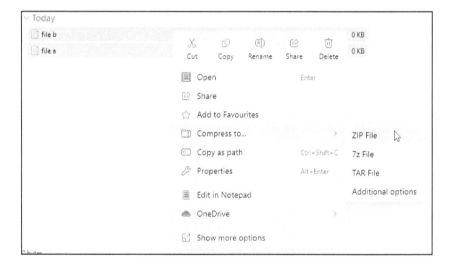

4. Select the type of extension, such as ZIP, 7Z, TAR (see Additional Options in the next paragraph).
5. The compressed file you just created will open; rename it if needed.

Additional Options

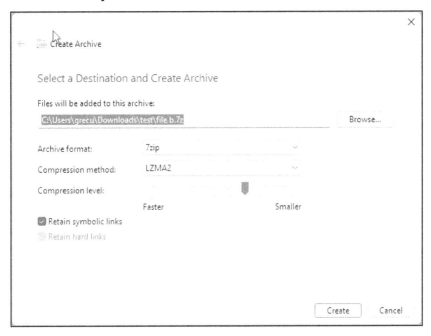

You can call up the **Create Archive** screen by selecting the Additional Options item in step 4. Inside you will find:

-   **Directory Field**: for entering the path and name of the compressed file.
-   **Archive Format:** list of formats that can be created.

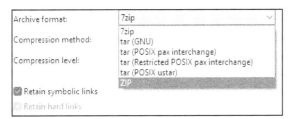

-   **Compression method:** specific to the format chosen earlier.
-   **Compression level:** based on the speed of creation or desired archive size.

How to extract a compressed archive (ZIP, 7Z, TAR)

If you have a compressed archive, you can extract it, that is, unpack it and copy the files to a folder.

1. Right click on the compressed file.
2. Click on **Extract all...** A window will open, allowing you to choose the destination path.
3. Click **Extract**.

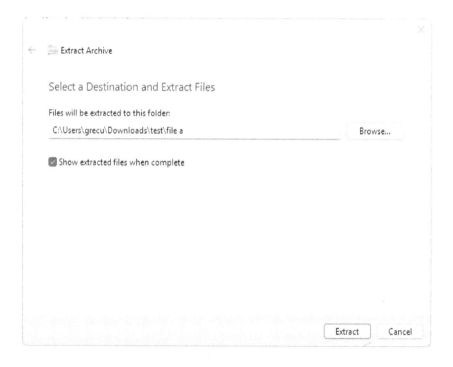

How to use the Widgets

Widgets is a feature that allows you to quickly access information directly from your desktop without opening separate applications. *It's often the screen that pops up unintentionally...* with the news, weather and more.

To open the Widget panel, locate the icon in the bottom left corner (usually the icon represents the weather, traffic or its icon) or type the combination of keys Windows + W.

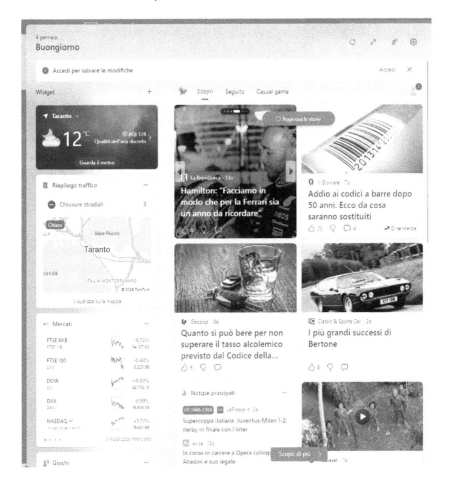

How to customize the widgets

1. In the upper right you can find the settings icon. Clicking on it will open the customization panel.

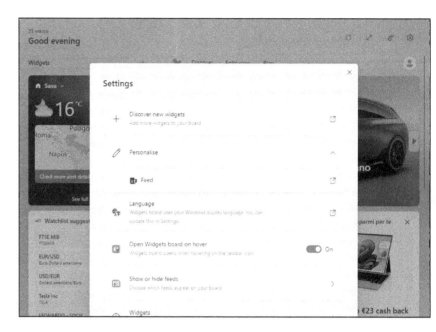

2. By clicking on the **Discover new Widgets** section, you can add new widgets from the online store

How to uninstall a program

When you run out of disk space or there are problems with an application, you may need to uninstall it. Uninstalling a program involves removing all its components, including associated files, settings and data.

1. Go to Settings.
2. Click on **Apps** on the left.
3. Click on **Installed Apps.**
4. Select the application youw ant to remove and click Uninstall.

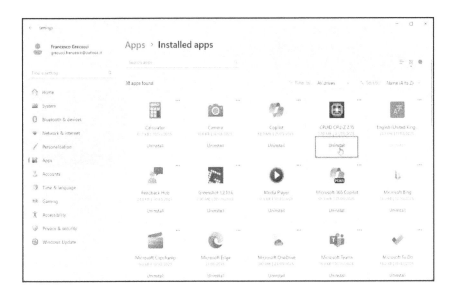

Virtual and Physical CD/DVD devices

How to mount and unmount an .ISO file

ISO files emulate optical CD/DVD-ROM media and can be **mounted** to access their contents, simulating the insertion of a disc into the drive. In Windows 11, this feature is built into the operating system, so you don't need to install any additional software.

1. Open File Explorer and locate the directory containing the ISO file.
2. Double-click on the file if File Explorer is the default application. If not, right click and on the menu that appears click on **Mount**.

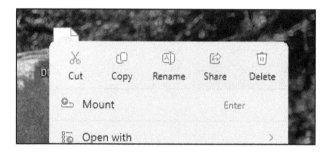

3. In the left panel of the File Explorer on the left you will see a CD/DVD-ROM drive. To unmount (remove the media) simply right-click on the drive and click **Eject**.

How to burn an .ISO file

To burn the contents of a virtual disk image on a physical medium, simply follow this procedure using Windows.

1. Select the ISO image you want to burn.
2. Right click, select Show more options, and then select the Burn disc image option.
3. Select the drive you want to use and click on the Burn button. Of course, you will need to insert the appropriate media type into the burner. For example, if the image exceeds 4.7GB, you will need to use an 8.5GB double-layer DVD.

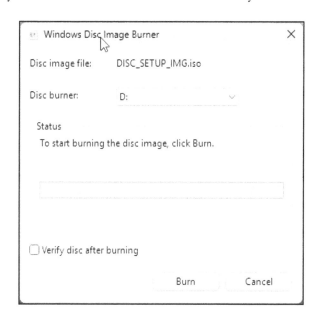

Device Manager

At the beginning of this book, we talked about Device Manager: this component of Windows allows you to view and manage all your computer's hardware devices, organized into categories. It also lets you update drivers, disable or uninstall devices, and diagnose problems using the information in each component's properties.

How to update a device's drivers

1. Open the Power User Menu (Windows + X combination or right-click on the Start button).
2. Click on Device Manager.
3. Select the device to update.

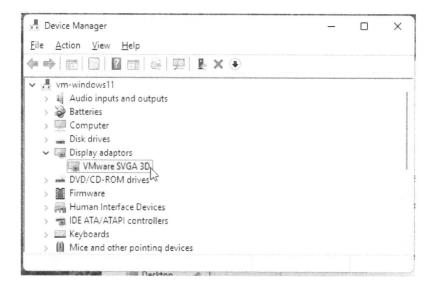

4. Right click and select Update Driver.

5. You can select whether to download driver updates from:
    a. **Automatic search:** Microsoft hosts a large database of device drivers.

If Windows determines that the latest drivers are already installed, you can click on Search for updated drivers on Windows Update. The system will search for the latest updates containing the correct drivers.

b. **Browse your computer:** If you have downloaded the drivers from the manufacturer's website, you can manually select them from the folder where they were saved.

How to disable (and enable) a device

1. Open the Power User Menu (Windows + X key combination or right-click on the Start button).
2. Click on Device Manager.
3. Select the device to disable.
4. Click on Disable Device.

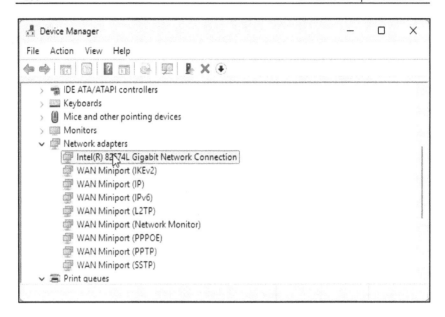

To reactivate the device, repeat the procedure.

The device will not be usable when is disabled. Disabling essential devices in your system may make it unstable. Be cautios when disabling and uninstalling devices.

Uninstall device drivers

1. Open the Power User Menu (Windows + X key combination or right-click on the start button).
2. Click on Device Manager.
3. Select the device you want to uninstall.
4. Click on Uninstall Device.
5. Click Uninstall again to confirm the operation.

This will completely remove the drivers and the device's system interface. This is usually used to reinstall drivers with other drivers in case of malfunctions or problems.

How to reinstall drivers

Once uninstalled, the device will be categorized as undefined and uncategorized. The system will treat it as though it's a newly connected device.

1. Search for the uninstalled device: right-click on the name of your PC and click on Scan for hardware change.

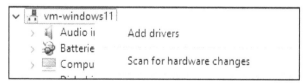

2. As mentioned earlier, the newly removed device will appear as an unknown device, meaning a detected device that lacks installed drivers.

3. If everything goes well the system will reinstall the drivers
    again.

Be careful when uninstalling device drivers. Drivers are critical for your
system's stability, especially when dealing with essential devices.

Network and Internet

How to turn your PC into a Wi-Fi hotspot

Windows 11 can function as an ideal Wi-Fi access point. A simple computer with Ethernet and Wireless connectivity is enough to share the connection with up to 8 devices. To configure it, you need a network name and password, as well as the Internet connection to share with other devices.

> An **access point (AP)** is a network device that allows wireless devices to connect to a wired network using Wi-Fi. Access points extend the range of a wireless network, serving as a link between the wired network and wireless devices like laptops, smartphones, and tablets.

1. Open Settings.
2. On the left click on Network & Internet.
3. Click on Mobile Hotspot.
4. Enable Mobile Hotspot.
5. Under Share my internet connection from, select the source of your internet connection (e.g., Wi-Fi or Ethernet).
6. Click Edit to customize the network name, password and band (2.4 GHz or 5Ghz).
7. You can now connect your devices to the new wireless network.

How to connect to a Wi-Fi network

Connecting to a wireless network is very simple with Windows 11. Make sure to have the security key ready in case it's a protected network!

1. Open the quick settings at the bottom right . If the PC is not connected to the internet, the typically appears as a globe with a cross.

2. Click on the arrow to the right of the Wi-Fi icon.

3. Select the Wireless access point and click Connect. You can also press the WPS button on your router to connect automatically, otherwise enter the password. If no networks appear, click the Wi-Fi button to activate the connection. If you are on a notebook, there might also be a physical switch to activate the network card.

How to limit background data usage

Background traffic occurs unnoticed during PC activities. You can limit it, especially if you pay based on data consumption. It's also a way to increase network performance.

1. Open Settings.
2. Click on **Network and Internet**.
3. Click on **Advanced network settings**.
4. Click on **Data usage**.
5. Click on **Enter Limit** to define the limit of data consumption
6. Compared to Windows 10, you can now define your own custom limit.
   a. **Limit type:** daily, weekly, monthly, one time or unlimited.
   b. **Day on which to reset the limit.**
   c. **MB or GB data limit** (1 GB = 1024 MB).

Geeks Space

Tutorials for advanced users and emergency situations

Author's note

Many of the procedures you'll read in the following pages are exclusively dedicated to Windows 11 Pro, Enterprise, and Education editions. If you're not familiar with the differences between the various versions, Appendix A includes a summary and comparison table for reference.

Recovery Drive

The recovery key is a support for installing Windows. In addition, it allows you to fix various problems with your system, including:

- **Windows startup issues:** if your PC does not boot properly, you can use the flash drive to access recovery options.
- **System Restore:** restore Windows to factory settings or a prior restore point (e.g., your system from two days ago) without losing your personal files.
- **Troubleshooting:** various tools to diagnose and resolve boot problems, repair system errors and manage recovery options.
- **Reinstall Windows from scratch.**

How to make a recovery drive

The capacity of the drive must be at least 16GB. All data on the drive will be erased.

1. Connect the flash drive to the PC.
2. Type inside of the Search taskbar **Create a recovery drive.**
3. Follow the on-screen instructions.
4. Choose the connected USB drive as the target device.
5. Start the process of creating the USB stick.

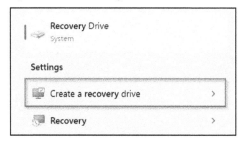

Post-installation

How to check for Windows updates

Windows 11 frequently performs sizable updates. Because these updates are done in the background, the process may often be interrupted unexpectedly for various reasons. In other cases, the operating system accumulates updates, requiring manual intervention to download them. This occurs mainly after the installation of Windows. Therefore, it is advisable to pay attention and complete the updates before installing any applications.

1. Go to Settings.
2. Click on Windows Update from the left menu.
3. Press the Check for updates button and check that the label You're up to date is present.

4. If this is not the case, there are pending updates, click on Install or, in any case, allow it to proceed automatically. You may be asked to restart your PC.

Do this periodically or in case you notice that your PC is slowing down for no apparent reason.

How to install a printer or a scanner

With the updated Windows 11 settings, installing printers is simple. You only need to allow the operating system to find drivers.

1. Open Settings.
2. Click on **Bluetooth & Devices**, on the left panel.
3. Click on **Printers & Scanners**.

4. Click on **Add Device**.

5. The system will now detect all the printers connected to your network or directly to your PC. So, connect the printer/scanner/multifunction to your PC via network (wireless or ethernet) or USB cable.
6. Once detected, click **Add Device** next to the printer or scanner detected.

If the printer is not detected automatically

If the network printer has already been connected and configured or is connected to the PC via USB and turned on but nothing appears, click Add a device manually.

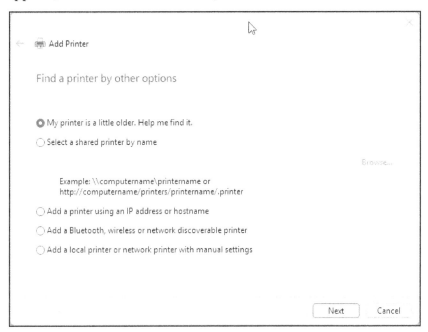

The Add Printer window shows several options to configure the printer.

- **My printer is a little older. Help me find it.** Windows will attempt another search; if no devices are found, it will return to the previous screen.
- **Select a shared printer by name.** Enter the printer path (as shown in the example) in the text box, or click on Browse... to navigate between shared devices if a PC is currently sharing the printer.
- **Add a printer using an IP address or hostname.** If you know the local network name of the printer or its IP address *(if you're unsure what this is, refer to the section on networks in this book)*, enter it into the text box that appears.
- **Add a Bluetooth, wireless or network discoverable printer.** Performs a search similar to the first point.
- **Add a local printer or network printer with manual settings.** Allows manual configuration of the printer via parallel (LPT), serial (COM), or network settings.

How to manually set-up a network printer

I often configure shared network printers by using the final point of the paragraph in a simple manner, if installing them normally or double-clicking on the share in File Explorer does not work properly.

1. I simulate it as an local printer using the LPT1 port and I install it.

2. Reopen the **Printers & Scanner** option panel.
3. I click on the new printer.
4. Then, I click on Printer Properties.

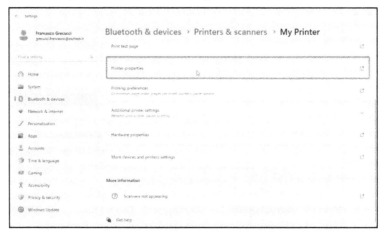

5. I go inside the tab **Ports**.

6. Click on **Add Port...** and then on **Local Port.**

7. I add the share name \\192.168.1.100\printer.

8. I click on OK.
9. This method successfully configures a network printer manually.

Boost your performance

How to delete temporary files

Temporary files are similar to paper towels: once used by the system or applications, they often linger in memory, piling up as unnecessary clutter.

How to show hidden items

1. Open File Explorer.
2. On top, click on View.

3. Under the Show menu, click on Hidden Items.

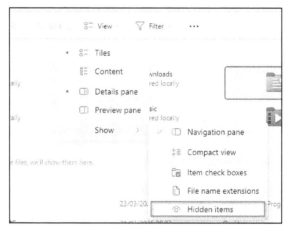

Without this setting enabled it is impossible to find the folder of temporary files!

Delete temporary files in user folder

1. Open File Explorer.
2. Navigate to the following path:
   C:\Users\YourName\AppData\Local\Temp
3. Select all files inside and delete them

4. Check the Do this for all current items option and click on Continue. Ensure you have administrator privileges to delete temporary files.

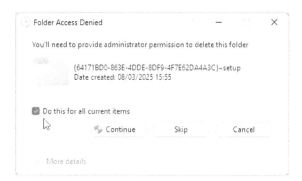

5. Click on Skip (check another time Do this for all current items) to ignore the deletion of files still needed by running programs.

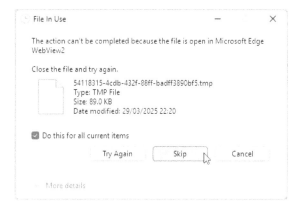

6. This must be repeated for each user of the PC.

Delete temporary system files

1. Open File Explorer.
2. Go into this path C:\Windows\Temp.
3. Follow steps 3, 4, and 5 mentioned earlier

Your File Explorer doesn't show AppData Folder?

You have to enable the Hidden items view in File Explorer to show the hidden files list.

1. Open File Explorer.
2. On the top, click on View.
3. Go into the Show menu.
4. Enable Hidden Items.

It's recommended to disable this setting after deleting temporary files.

What to do if your PC is slow to load files

If after some time your computer starts to slow down, it is absolutely **normal**. Daily use, updates, and **file fragmentation** cause ever-increasing slowdowns as time goes by. Fragmentation is the possibility that each file that is created will be split into several parts and spread throughout the hard disk. It is clear that to read or write the file, this will be taken piece by piece each time. In addition, the hard disk may encounter **sector failure**, so it will take more time to try to read the data correctly. Fortunately, with a little cleaning and good **defragmentation** the problem can be solved. Be aware, however, that after a few years and certain read/write cycles your hard drive may have undergone its normal aging and will need to be replaced.

First of all: do a backup

First, to prevent data loss in case of hard disk failure, make a copy on external media or on the Cloud of your most important data.

Perform the System Cleaning

Programs like **CCleaner**, **Clean Master** or CleanMyPC can relieve your computer from any temporary files, cookies, histories and much more of the hindrance to your hard disk. A lighter disk (this is especially true for SSDs) also means a more agile disk when searching for files.

Is it easier for you to grope in a room full of clothes, boxes, underwear and empty ice cream trays or in a clean one with everything in its place?

Do an Error Checking

1. In File Explorer, right-click on the partition where you are experiencing the slowdown. If there is more than one, you will need to do this on each partition.
2. Click on Properties.

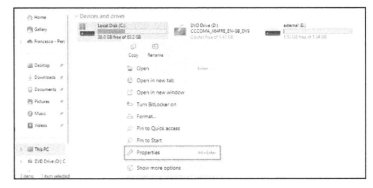

3. In the window that will open, go to the Tools tab;
4. Click the Check button.

Long-time users may recognize this tool as the classic **ScanDisk** *utility.*

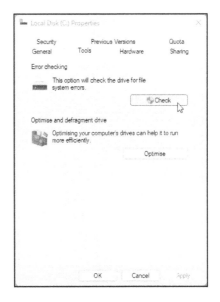

▶ Don't use only Windows tools!

Utilities such as CrystalDiskInfo, Hard Disk Sentinel and Ashampoo HDD Control 3, of which the first is free, check the condition of your hard drive or solid-state drive. These programs can determine how healthy the device is and how long the disks have before their life cycle comes to an end

How to defragment and optimize drive

Files are fragmented when a document is deleted. Each deleted file is replaced by another, which may not have the same size. It is clear that to find space in addition to the previously written file, you will need to do so in separate areas of the disk. This will cause, at the time of use of the file, a continuous movement of the hard disk head, which must search for scattered file fragments.. Fortunately, there is **defragmentation**. This operation allows you to rearrange the files to put them in order and avoid this bad situation.

1. Inside the Search bar on the bottom of the screen, type Optimise Drives.

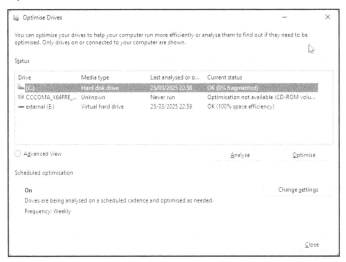

2. Click on Analyse after selecting the drive to optimise. Once the analysis is complete, click on Optimise.

Defragmentation is a process of reorganizing data on a traditional hard disk drive (HDD) to improve data access speed and system performance. However, when it comes to solid-state drives (SSDs), the situation is different. SSDs use a different technology compared to HDDs and do not benefit from traditional defragmentation. In fact, defragmenting an SSD can reduce its lifespan since SSDs have a limited number of write cycles. Windows 11 optimizes SSDs without requiring traditional defragmentation. The end user only needs to click on Optimize, and Windows will take care of the rest!

How to remove startup items

Windows 11 has improved the function for removing unnecessary programs at startup, inserting it directly in Task Manager without going through the `msconfig` command. There are numerous programs at startup that our PC needs: antivirus, video card drivers, printer control software etc. but also unnecessary programs. If you know which applications you don't want to start at startup, here's what to do to remove them:

1. Open Task Manager.

2. Open the **Startup Apps** tab (you can easily find it by searching the dashboard icon). Inside you will find every program that is currently opened at startup. Be careful about what you will disable from the startup! You might unintentionally deactivate critical applications, like antivirus software or video card drivers

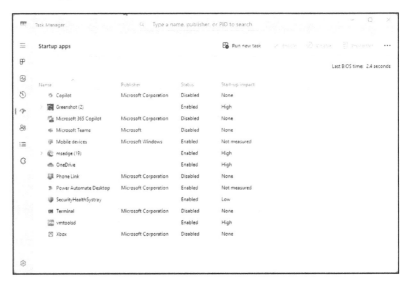

3. To disable a startup program, select it and click **Disable** at the top.
4. Of course, to test the effective changes, you will need to reboot your PC.

How to disable unnecessary graphical effects

If you want to speed up your PC without taking into account the graphical effects of the operating system, you can easily disable them and leave only the essential, such as the shading of characters (disabling it would make the text difficult to read, tiring eyes).

1. Open the Power User Menu (Windows + X key combination or right-click on start button) and click on the **System** menu item.
2. Under **Related links**, click on Advanced System Settings.

3. Under Performance, click on Settings.

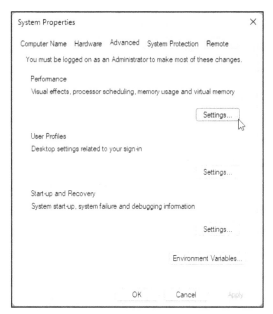

4. Disable the following options:
   - Animate controls and elements inside windows
   - Animate windows when minimising and maximising
   - Animations in the taskbar
   - Fade out menu items after clicking
   - Fade or slide menus into views
   - Fade or slide ToolTips into view

- Show shadows under mouse pointer
- Show shadows under windows
- Show translucent selection rectangle
- Slide open combo boxes
- Save taskbar thumbnail preview
- Use drop shadows for icon labels on the desktop

5. Press OK to confirm.

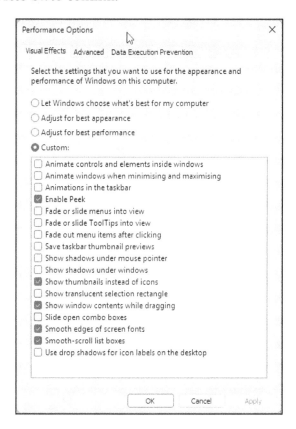

How to assign a graphic card to an application

In PCs with dual graphics cards, Windows has a feature that forces a program to use the video card of your choice. It often happens that the application chooses the wrong one, not taking full advantage of the graphics processing capabilities of the dedicated GPU of superior performance. With this setting, you can finally solve this problem. You can also save energy by removing applications that do not need high performance (or to split the load) and assigning them the integrated video card.

1. Open Settings.
2. On the left, click on System;
3. Inside the Display section, click on Graphics.

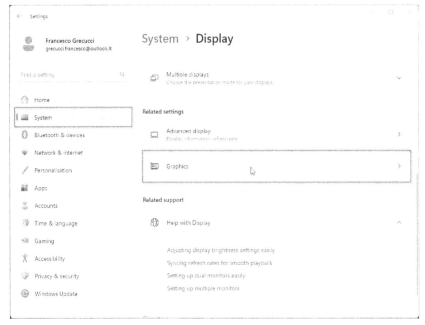

6. Use the drop-down menu to select whether to configure a traditional application or a Microsoft Store app.

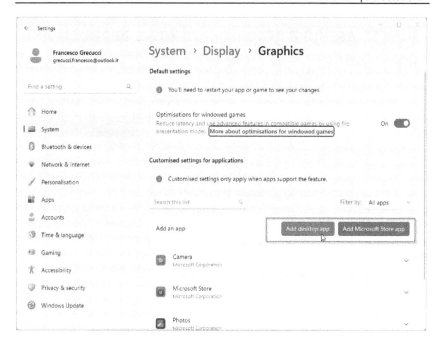

4. Search and select the application.
5. On **GPU Preference**, select **Power Saving** or **High Performance**.

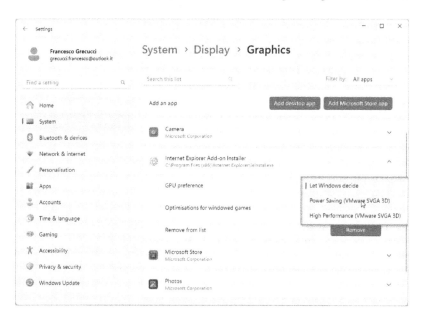

System Registry

The Microsoft Windows registry stores all the settings and variables necessary for the proper functioning of the programs. For example, the registry allows Windows to store your chosen background and the folder where Microsoft Office is installed. The parameters within the register are strictly organized by category and, in the case of applications, also by developer. This way, Windows is able to quickly retrieve the configuration information needed to run programs properly. The access and modification of this database is also allowed by the computer administrator.

> **Caution:** changing even a single character without proper knowledge can make your PC unusable, so **be very careful.**

The program that manages the registry is the Registry Editor, better known as **REGEDIT** because of the command that runs it. You can start the Registry Editor, by writing REGEDIT into the Search bar.

Keys

Once opened, the editor will show several folders, named **Keys**. The main ones, from which all the others branch out, are:

1. **HKEY_CLASSES_ROOT:** contains information about the user interface, links and drag & drop. Entering this section of the registry, you will find a list of all file extensions stored, each linked to the default program used to open it.

2. **HKEY_CURRENT_USER:** collects information about the user who has accessed the registry editor. These are parameters limited to the profile you are using. It is divided into several main subkeys, such as:

    *   **AppEvents:** contains the sounds and labels associated with various system events (empty trash, take screenshots, etc.)
    *   **Control Panel:** contains the settings entered in the control panel.

- **Environment:** the environment variables that can be modified in the System panel.

- **Keyboard Layout:** contains information on the keyboard.

- **Network:** Stores settings for mapped network drivers (for example, Z: links to \\192.168.0.100\Shared).

- **Printers:** Contains details about installed printers and the default printer.

- **Software:** contains the program configurations related to the current user.

3. **HKEY_LOCAL_MACHINE:** is commonly referenced in tutorials, as it stores system-wide software settings and hardware configurations for all users, and is divided into:

   a. **Hardware:** information on ports and hardware.

   b. **Software:** settings for installed software.

   c. **System:** startup parameters and driver information.

4. **HKEY_USERS:** information and parameters of each user stored in the computer. The subkeys are nothing more than the contents of the **HKEY_CURRENT_USER** of every other user. So, you do not need to go into the other profiles to change their settings.

5. **HKEY_CURRENT_CONFIG:** data on current hardware.

Registry Editor.

How to reach a key

The registry keys shown in the tutorials are real paths to follow. For example, to reach the key related to the parameters of installed programs the string will be as follows:
HKEY_LOCAL_MACHINE\SOFTWARE
simply copy it into the address bar at the top.

Path to the key.

Values

Each key contains **values**, which are settings in various formats, such as numeric, string, or binary that make up the actual setting. For example, the desktop background path might appear as a string value like: "C:\Users\Michael\Pictures\Wallpaper.PNG".

Values		
ID	Type	Description
0	REG_NONE	No type value

1	REG_SZ	String value (character set)
2	REG_EXPAND_SZ	Expandable string value
3	REG_BINARY	Binary data
4	REG_DWORD	32-bit numeric value (maximum 4,294,967,295) little-endian
5	REG_DWORD_BIG_ENDIAN	32-bit numeric value big-endian
6	REG_LINK	Link to another registry key
7	REG_MULTI_SZ	Multi-string value consisting of an ordered set of strings
8	REG_RESOURCE_LIST	Resource list (used in Plug and Play)
9	REG_FULL_RESOURCE_DESCRIPTOR	Resource descriptor (used in Plug and Play)
10	REG_RESOURCE_REQUIREMENT_LIST	Resource requirement list (used in Plug and Play)
11	REG_QWORD	64-bit numeric value

Export the registry file

The export of the registry consists in a backup copy to prevent that the changes made can create damage without being able to go back. Just save a copy and then reload it and make everything go back as before.

Of course, this does not mean that you can do everything you want without consequences, especially if it causes damage that prevents the system from booting and resetting.

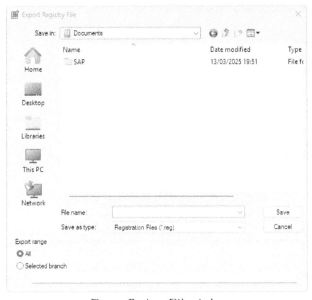

Export Registry File window

1. Click on **File** > **Export**.
2. Select **All**, at the bottom of the **Export Range** panel.
3. Save the file to external storage or cloud storage

System Informations

Checking the status of the system is essential. > Knowing about installed components like .NET Framework and DirectX can be invaluable in solving problems that would otherwise seem impossible to solve.

System Information

System Information is a Windows tool that provides a complete overview of your PC: details about the installed components, amount of RAM, CPU power and much more. It also allows you to check installed drivers, network connections, print jobs and more. You can find it easily by using the search box.

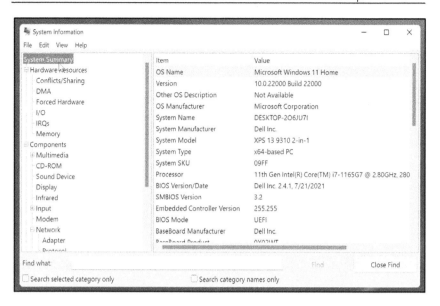

GrecTech SysInfo

Grectech SysInfo is a free software designed to provide a complete analysis of your system, including detailed information about the hardware components, drivers and installed software. The program automatically detects your operating system and displays all relevant information.

Among its main features, Grectech SysInfo allows you to view details about the hardware, such as the CPU, motherboard, graphic card, RAM and hard disk. It also provides in-depth information about the installed drivers, including version and manufacturer, and software on your system, such as name, version and manufacturer.

The software is easy to use and has an intuitive interface that allows users to easily navigate between different sections to access the information they want. It is also possible to export the collected data into a simple text file, facilitating sharing or archiving.

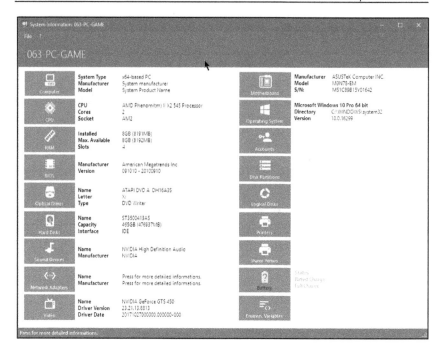

You can download it at this link

https://www.majorgeeks.com/files/details/grectech_sysinf
o.html

How to check the installed versions of .NET Framework

.NET Framework is a set of components developed by Microsoft. This allowed the realization of programming languages (Visual C++, Visual C#, Visual Basic .NET) that use .NET to build applications and games. Several versions of this package have been released over the years, some already in Windows.

How to detect installed versions from 1.0 to 4.0

To detect which .NET Framework version from 1.0 to 4.0 is installed, follow this procedure:

1. Open the registry editor (*regedit*);
2. Navigate to this path

> HKEY_LOCAL_MACHINE\SOFTWARE\Microsoft\NET
> Framework Setup\NDP

3. Within the NDP key (or folder), you will find all the installed versions ranging from 1.0 to 4.0.

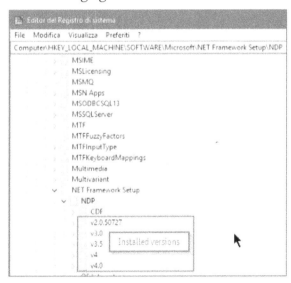

How to detect versions 4.0 and later

1. In the Registry Editor, type (or search for):

```
HKEY_LOCAL_MACHINE\SOFTWARE\Microsoft\.NETFramewor
k\v4.0.30319\SKUs
```

2. Within the SKUs key, all versions of .NET Framework later than 4.0 installed on the PC are listed.

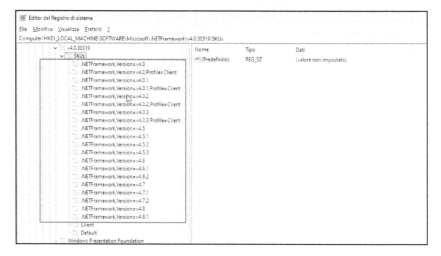

How to check the version of DirectX installed on your computer

DirectX is a package of runtime libraries designed to enable the development of multimedia applications, in particular games, on the Windows platform. DirectX provides features and services that simplify the development of multimedia applications, such as 2D and 3D graphics rendering, sound processing and device input. In addition, DirectX has a significant impact on game performance as it optimizes the hardware and software of the graphics card and processor. When developers create games with DirectX, they will use a specific version of the DirectX API. The end user who wants to run the game must install the corresponding version of DirectX. Typically, the latest version of DirectX is released at the same time as the Windows operating system. For example, Windows 11 includes DirectX 12, which is the latest version.

The update can lead to significant performance improvements in games, thanks to the improved graphics and audio processing found in new versions. However, updating DirectX is not always necessary because many games include a specific version of DirectX required for that game.

1. Search **dxdiag** in the Search field in the taskbar.
2. Click on **No** if it requires control of the driver's digital signature.
3. In the **DirectX Version** label you will find the API version.

You can save the displayed information in a text file by clicking on
Save All Information...

How to check how much RAM your PC has

Everything running on your computer - windows, icons, programs, and files-temporarily resides in RAM. **RAM is the temporary memory of your computer, used to hold everything that is running.** Let's use an old cabinet as an example. Imagine this drawing drawn on the screen. Where does it reside at that given time? In RAM!

The programmers of the time had to make considerable efforts to try to contain everything within a memory of very low capacity compared to that of modern computers. **From this it follows that: the more RAM you have, the better your PC is.** It will be faster, yes, but above all it will be able to handle several operations at the same time without slowdowns.

A modern PC generally needs to have these ranges of RAM in order to run at its best:

Type of use	Recommended RAM
Office/home use	8-16 GB
Graphic production	16-32 GB
Video production	16-32 GB
3D production	32-64 GB

Just to make a comparison, in 2014, the recommended RAM was this

Type of use	Recommended RAM
Office/home use	4-8 GB
Graphic production	8-16 GB
Video production	8-16 GB
3D production	16-32GB

In 2004 we were at much lower values...

Type of use	Recommended RAM
Office/home use	512 MB* – 1 GB
Graphic production	1-2 GB
Video production	1-2 GB
3D production	2-4 GB

* 512 MB equals 0.5 GB

To check how much RAM your PC has:

1. Open the Power User Menu (**Windows + X** key combination or right-click on the Start button).
2. On the left, click on System.
3. Check the value in the Installed RAM label.

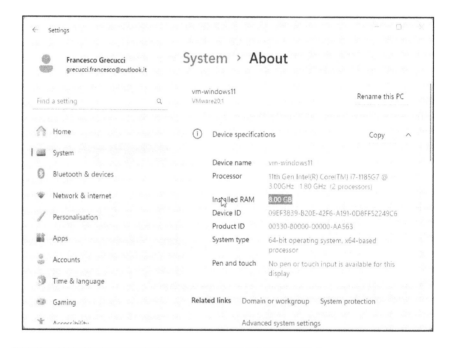

What does Usable mean?

Not all the installed memory is dedicated exclusively to operating system and application usage. **RAM can be shared by some hardware devices that take a portion of it to work, such as some built-in graphic chips.**

Video cards can be integrated or dedicated. In the first case, there is a chip on the motherboard (the main logic board) that manages the generation of images and uses the same RAM as the computer. In the second case, there is a separate graphic card, connected to the motherboard, with its own chip and RAM memory dedicated exclusively to the management of visual elements.

How to check which CPU is installed in your PC

The heart, indeed the brain of a PC, is the CPU (Central Processing Unit), that is the component that performs all the calculations and allows the system to work.

The power and performance of a CPU depend on several key factors.

1. **Number of cores**: the more cores a CPU has, the more operations it can perform simultaneously. Multi-core processors (such as dual-core (2), quad-core (4), octa-core (8), hexa-core (16)) are able to handle multiple tasks simultaneously, improving overall performance.
2. **Clock Speed:** is measured in GHz (Gigahertz), represents the number of operations the CPU performs per second. The higher the clock speed, the more instructions are processed by the CPU in a given time period.
3. **Cache:** cache memory is a very high-speed short-term memory used to store data frequently used by the CPU. çarger cache improves performance, as the CPU accesses data faster without relying on RAM (remember the bottleneck?).
4. **Manufacturing process:** the manufacturing process, measured in nanometers (nm), affects the density of transistors in the CPU. Processors built with smaller nanometer technologies tend to have better performance and energy efficiency.

All these parameters, and many more specific ones, are collected in the data sheet of your CPU. But how do I know which processor it is?

1. Open the Power User Menu (Windows + X key combination or right-click on the Start button) and click on System.
2. Inside the Processor section you will find brand, model and clock frequency.

How to check the size of the system disk (and other installed disks)

A PC may have one or more Hard Disk drivers or SSDs installed. They are listed with the letters of the alphabet starting from C: onwards. Generally, the disk where Windows is saved and most of the programs is the drive C:.

Where are A and B?

To answer this question we must go back in time. In MS-DOS systems and early versions of Windows, the drive letters A: and B: were reserved for floppy disks.

In fact, before the PC could also not have a hard disk, or at least an SSD (the first solid-state disks marketed are from 2006 onwards), but start directly from floppy.

31 Workbench system boot floppy disk for Commodore Amiga

Hard Disk or SSD?

The main difference between a HDD (Hard Disk Drive) and a SSD (Solid State Drive) is the technology used to store and retrieve data. The first uses rotating magnetic plates to store data and a read/write head to access the data contained in these plates. It is slower than an SSD, but provides greater storage capacity. The second uses a NAND flash memory to store data, without moving parts. It is more expensive in relation to capacity but more durable and reliable, having no moving parts that can fail.

HDDs are great for storing large amounts of data at low cost, SSDs offer superior performance and reliability, making them ideal for operating systems and applications that require fast read and write operations.

32 A Hard Disk viewed from the inside reveals the magnetic disks and the read/write head. https://www.pexels.com/it-it/foto/silver-hard-drive-interals-33278/

*33*Two 1TB (1024GB) NVMe-type SSDs. Thanks to Andrey Matveev:
https://www.pexels.com/it-it/foto/ssd-nvme-ad-alte-prestazioni-su-superficie-grigia-28666524/

To know how big your PC's disk is:

1. Open the Power User Menu (Windows + X key combination or right-click on the Start button).
2. Click on **Disk Management**;
3. Once open, you will see a list of all installed drives, their sizes, and partition details

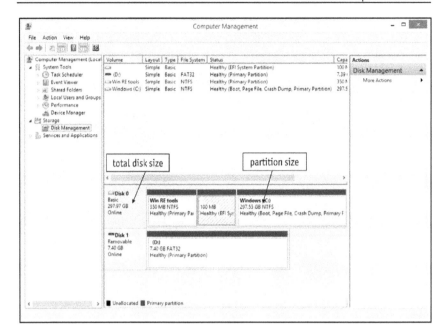

As you can see from the screen above, the disk can be partitioned in several parts. You can, in fact, choose to partition any mass storage drive like hard disk, SSD, USB flash drives, SD-Card, etc.

The system disk is usually partitioned by Windows during installation, in fact those small partitions are needed to run the system.

How to partition a disk

To partition a disk into multiple sections, you can shrink the single partition that comprises it.

> When partitioning a drive, there is always a risk of data loss, especially if anything goes wrong in the process. It is good to do it on an empty disk or, in any case, make a backup first.

Per fare ciò:

1. Open the Power User Menu (Windows + X key combination or right-click on start button).
2. Open Disk Management.
3. **Shrink volume:** Right-click on the partition you want to resize and select Shrink volume.

Enter the size in megabytes (MB) you want to allocate to the new partition and click on Shrink.

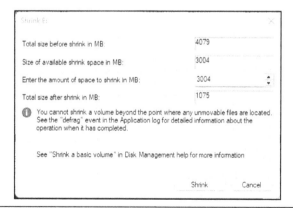

> To convert from GB to MB, divide the desired amount by 1024.
> For example, 20GB will be 20480MB.

4. **Create a new partition:** Right-click on the newly created unallocated area and click on **New simple volume.**

2.93 GB
Unallocated

New Simple Volume...

10. **Assign parameters to the partition:** assign drive letter,
    name and format (i.e. initialize and create actual space) the
    new partition. This will be done through the Volume
    Wizard.

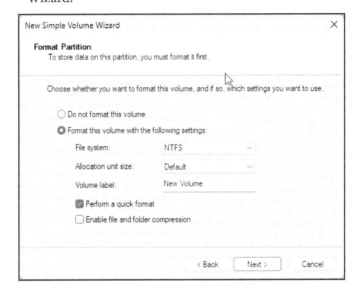

How to change letter of a storage unit or a partition

Windows identifies mass storage drives using alphabetical letters. Typically, the pattern is as follows:

Letter	Generally assigned device
A: B:	Floppy Disk Drives
C:	System Drive (where Windows is generally installed)
D: E: F:	Internal and External Drives (Hard Disks, USB Keys, SD Cards etc.)
X: Y: Z:	CD/DVD Drives

If, for example, you do not want the internal drive to be assigned to letter E: and the USB stick to letter D:, you can reverse them. When you do this, always close all files and programs to avoid data loss, as they will always access the old drive reference (for example, F:\2022\ introduction.doc).

1. Open the Power User Menu (Windows + X key combination or right-click on start button).
2. Select Disk Management.
3. Select the drive whose letter you want to change.
4. Right click and select the item Change Drive Letter and Paths...
5. Click on Change....

6. From the drop-down menu select a letter and click OK.

How to view GPU activity in Task Manager

▶ Inside the Task Manager, you can see which process is using the GPU engine in the **Processes** tab.

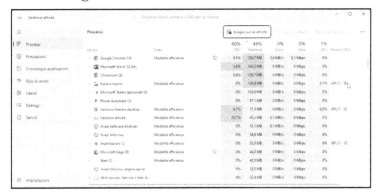

▶ By going to the Performance tab and selecting an installed GPU (Windows 11, in fact, shows the data related to the usage of each individual video card) you can access a lot of useful information.

If the GPU parameters are not visible in the Processes section of the Task Manager, right-click on the column header (e.g. right-click on Network) and enable the GPU and GPU Engine columns.

42% Memory	0% Disk	0% Netwc	
			Type
			✓ Status
			Publisher
50.7 MB	0.1 MB/s	0 ME	PID
			Process name
			Command line
6.2 MB	0 MB/s	0 ME	✓ CPU
143.2 MB	0 MB/s	0 ME	✓ Memory
3.2 MB	0 MB/s	0 ME	✓ Disk
2.4 MB	0 MB/s	0 ME	✓ Network
			GPU
2.6 MB	0 MB/s	0 ME	GPU engine
1.3 MB	0 MB/s	0 ME	Power usage
19.8 MB	0 MB/s	0 ME	Power usage trend
1.3 MB	0 MB/s	0 ME	Resource values >

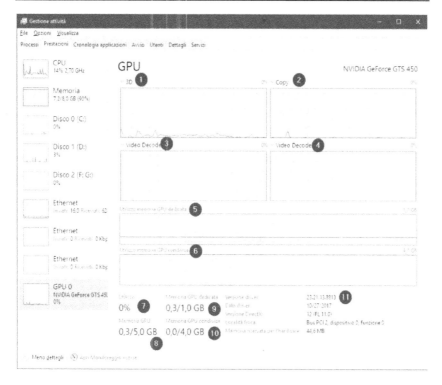

In the top right, you find the name of the video card. At the bottom, you will find:

1. Use of 3D rendering.
2. Use of Copy.
3. Hardware acceleration (encoder).
4. Hardware acceleration (decoder).
5. Dedicated GPU memory usage chart (the VRAM on the graphic card).
6. Shared GPU memory usage graph (the RAM of the PC offered to the video card).
7. The general use of GPU.
8. The total GPU memory (dedicated + shared) used compared to the maximum usable memory.
9. The RAM of the dedicated GPU used compared to the total.
10. The shared PC RAM used compared to the maximum usable.
11. Driver details including version, release date, DirectX compatibility, and hardware-reserved memory.

Networks and Remote Connections

IP Addresses and DNS

An IP address and a DNS must be defined for each network adapter (cable or wireless connection device). They are often assigned automatically by the modem/router, but can also be provided manually.

34 An ethernet port. This type of connection allows the network interface to connect to the cable network.

▶ What is an IP Address?

An IP (Internet Protocol) address is a sequence of 4 numbers that serves as a unique identifier. Each number ranges from 0 to 255. The IP address is used to identify your PC within your home or office network. It is used to transfer files from one PC to another or to communicate with the modem/router.

Knowing which internet node to send and receive data from is essential. Therefore, each device (computer, router, server, printer, etc.) must have its own unique IP.

IP addresses are divided into *public* and *private*. The private addresses are the identifiers I mentioned previously, used in the internal network, while the public ones are those assigned by the provider (the provider of the internet connection) to the modem/router to establish communication with external networks (and so, with the Internet). This device acts as a gateway by processing the requests of PCs within the network and sending them to various servers around the world. Servers must identify the recipient for sending information or the sender for receiving it. It follows that each modem/router or server must have its own unique IP.

The addresses mentioned earlier are IPv4 addresses. There are also newer IPv6 addresses, which are less common in home networks but longer and allow many more devices to be identified in a network.

▶ What is a DNS?

The DNS (Domain Name Service) is a service that allows the resolution of a host (network device) to its corresponding IP address. The DNS has an inverted tree hierarchical structure and is divided into domains (com, org, it, etc.). In few words: the DNS allows us to visit any website simply by calling it by name and not by IP address, which would be just a sequence of numbers. DNS is the translation from a name to an IP address.

How to change IP and DNS addresses

Within the network connections it is possible to have a picture of the situation on the parameters and the connection status of a network card.

1. Open Settings.
2. On the left, click on Network & Internet.
3. Click on the type of Network card (Ethernet if with wire, Wi-Fi for wireless connections).
4. Go to the section IP Assignment and click on Edit.

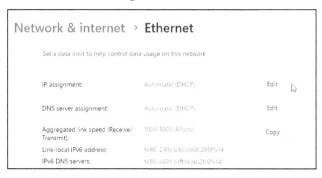

5. Switch to Manual.

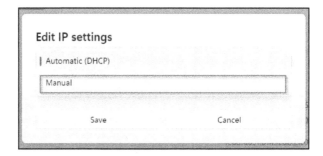

6. Select IPv4, or IPv6, or both and enter the IP address and DNS server parameters.

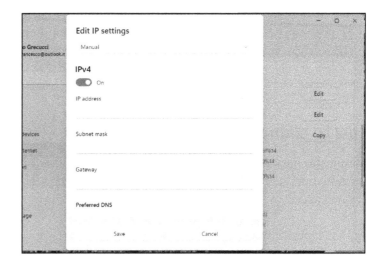

▶ **IP and DNS at a glance**

- **IPv4 address:** unique PC identifier on the local network.
- **IPv4 Subnet Mask:** parameter for local network subnets.
- **Default IPv4 gateway:** router IP address.
- **"IPv4 DNS Server:** references servers that translate domain names into IP addresses. If you do not know which one to enter, enter the same address as the router.

The same information can be obtained via command prompt by typing `ipconfig /all`.

If your PC sees other devices on the network but cannot browse the internet

▶ Verify that the gateway and DNS servers are correct.

▶ Check if there is internet connectivity from another device on the network.

▶ Check the router's connection by accessing its configuration panel through a browser at addresses like 192.168.1.1, 192.168.0.1, 192.168.1.254, or 192.168.0.254.

▶ Turn the network adapter off and back on.

▶ If you're on a Wi-Fi connection, make sure there is good signal coverage.

How to check Network Activity using Task Manager

1. Inside the **Processes** tab you can identify which process is utilizing the network.

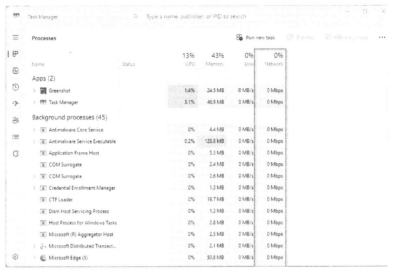

2. Then going to the **Performance** tab and clicking on one of the installed network cards (Windows 11, in fact, displays data regarding the usage of each individual network card) you can access a lot of useful information.

- **Send:** outgoing data traffic.
- **Receive:** incoming data traffic.
- **Adapter name:** the name of the network card.
- **DNS Name:** the complete name of the PC in the the network.
- **Connection type:** type of connection (Ethernet, Wi-Fi, etc.).
- **IPv4 address:** the IP address assigned to the network adapter using the IPv4 protocol.
- **IPv6 address:** the IP address assigned to the network adapter using the IPv6 protocol.

How to call another host on the network with PING command

The `ping` command sends test packets to a host (another PC or device on the network). The response from the host indicates whether communication is successful.

1. Start the command prompt;
2. Write:

```
ping hostname ip address
```

Where by *hostname* you mean the name of the PC to which you want to connect or the web server. For example:

```
ping www.google.it
```

3. If the connection is successful and the server is available, you will see an output like this:

4. If the server is down or there are connection issues, you will see a different output, as shown below:

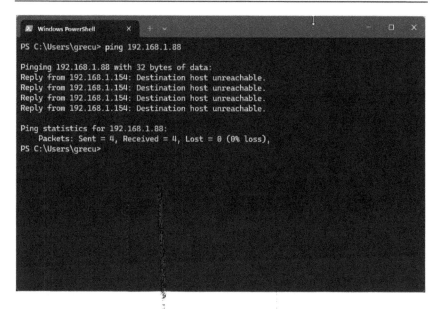

```
Windows PowerShell        ×    + ∨                                       −  □  ×

PS C:\Users\grecu> ping 192.168.1.88

Pinging 192.168.1.88 with 32 bytes of data:
Reply from 192.168.1.154: Destination host unreachable.
Reply from 192.168.1.154: Destination host unreachable.
Reply from 192.168.1.154: Destination host unreachable.
Reply from 192.168.1.154: Destination host unreachable.

Ping statistics for 192.168.1.88:
    Packets: Sent = 4, Received = 4, Lost = 0 (0% loss),
PS C:\Users\grecu>
```

Ping is one of the many diagnostic tools available from the command prompt, there are also:

- **Traceroute**: with the tracert command it traces all intermediate points between your PC and a remote server.
- **Netstat**: displays active network connections at the current time.
- **Pathping**: functions like tracert but provides much more detailed information. Takes longer to run the test as it also includes a ping at each node.
- **Getmac**: retrieves the unique MAC addresses of the network adapters installed on the PC.
- **Netsh:** Network shell, features various advanced commands, including `netsh wlan` for Wi-Fi configurations.

How to recover a wireless network password

If you accidentally lost a Wi-Fi key and have already connected to your PC at least once, you can still recover it. Windows securely stores them, but there is a way to retrieve them.. All you need is the command prompt and some commands to type.

1. At the prompt, type the following command and press Enter

```
netsh wlan show profile
```

```
C:\WINDOWS\system32\cmd.exe
Microsoft Windows [Versione 10.0.15063]
(c) 2017 Microsoft Corporation. Tutti i diritti sono riservati.

C:\Users\Francesco>netsh wlan show profile

Profili sull'interfaccia Wi-Fi:

Profili di Criteri di gruppo (sola lettura)
---------------------------------
    <Nessuno>

Profili utente
-------------
    Tutti i profili utente     : iPhone
    Tutti i profili utente     :
    Tutti i profili utente     :
    Tutti i profili utente     :
    Tutti i profili utente     :
    Tutti i profili utente     : Vodafone-WiFi
```

2. Take note of the network for which you need the password (for example Vodafone-WiFi) and write:

```
netsh            wlan            show            profile
name="networkname" key=clear
```

3. Go down until you find the `Key Content` item to see your Wi-Fi network access key. Inside the `Authentication` field, you can find the type of password required by the router or access point is also listed.

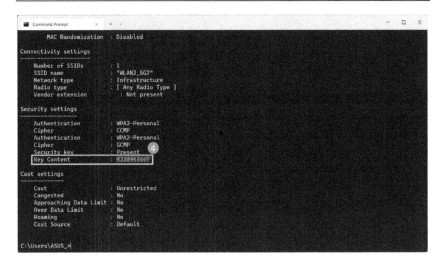

This procedure should only be used if the computer and wireless network are your property. I disclaim any responsibility for misuse of this procedure to recover Wi-Fi passwords.

How to join an Active Directory network

Active Directory provides a single point of reference, known as a **directory service**, for all objects within a network. This service is managed by one or more **Domain Controllers (DCs)**, which host a centralized database containing user information, such as **login credentials, permissions, and identity and security-related details**. In addition to user accounts, the database includes data about other network objects, such as computers, printers, and devices. Essentially, users can log in with their credentials and have access to their assigned resources from any PC within the local network, based on the permissions configured for them.

> Simply type the same username and password on any computer within your office network to access the same resources anywhere.

1. Open the Power User Menu (Windows + X key combination or right-click on start button) and click on System.
2. Go to About.
3. Under Related Links, click on Domain or Workgroup.

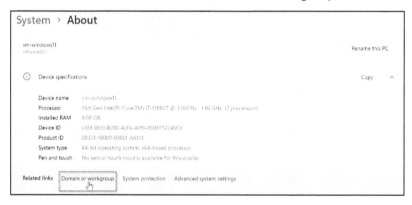

4. Click on Change...

5.   Check the **Domain** button and write your AD domain name.

6.   Digit the domain administrator username and password.
7.   If everything went fine, you would receive a message like Domain msdomain.
8.   Reboot the PC.

DNS Fix

In case the procedure returns an error instead of the above screen, try to assign the IP address of the Active Directory server as the primary DNS server.

How to add a VPN network

VPNs are private channels within the Internet network that connect to other private networks. Originally designed for the business world, they serve to unify the computer networks of multiple locations. They are also used to browse the Internet while masking one's tracks and pretending to be connected from another location. **Want an easy way to connect to your office's local network from home? The VPN is what you need!**

1. Open Settings.
2. Click on Network & Internet.
3. Click on VPN.

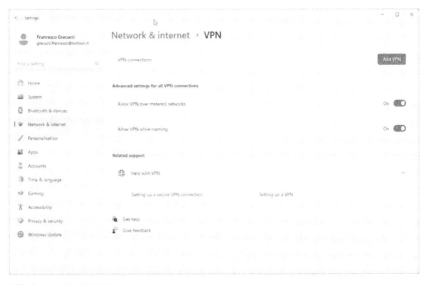

4. Click on Add VPN.
5. Enter the required parameters. These may include:
   - ▶ **VPN Provider**: Choose "Windows (built-in)" if you're using the built-in VPN client.
   - ▶ **Connection Name**: A name to identify your VPN connection.
   - ▶ **Server Address**: The address of the VPN server (e.g., an IP address or domain name).
   - ▶ **VPN Type**: Choose a protocol like PPTP, L2TP/IPsec, SSTP, or IKEv2.
   - ▶ **Authentication Method**: Choose how you'll authenticate (e.g., username/password, certificate, or pre-shared key).
   - ▶ **Username and Password**: If necessary, enter your credentials for the VPN.

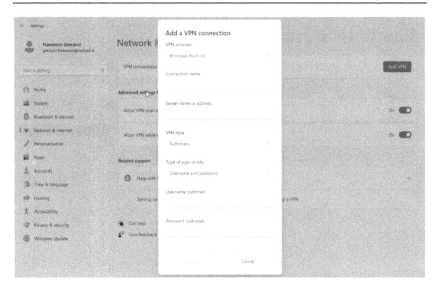

6. You will find the VPN in the quick settings (remember? Next to the date and system time).

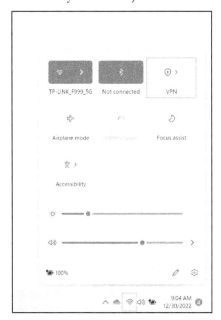

How to reactivate SMB1

Many Linux servers, NAS devices, and older Windows computers rely on an outdated file transfer protocol. This is the first version of SMB (read Samba), which allows you to connect to any computer on the network in a fairly simple way. The April 2018 release of Windows 10 deprecated it for security reasons If you need to communicate with a device that cannot update its protocol, refer to this guide. **Keep in mind that this procedure will reduce your PC's security.**

1. Open the Settings app;
2. Click System on the left bar.
3. Click on Optional Features.

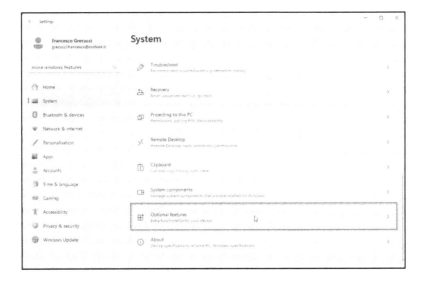

4. Scroll down to More Windows Features and click on it.
5. Check SMB 1.0/CIFS File Sharing Support

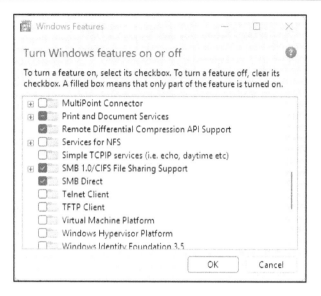

6. Reboot your PC if required.

How to enable remote connection

Remote Desktop Connection is an outstanding tool for connecting PCs remotely. However, it does not allow connections outside the LAN network unless a port 3389 is opened outward to only one of the computers on the network (very dangerous, it's more secure to use a VPN instead). It is, however, widely used both in the corporate and domestic sector. Before you start using it, you need to enable the remote computer to accept incoming connections.

1. Enter the **System** settings (you can easily search it in the Search field in Windows taskbar).

2. Click on **Advanced system settings.**

3. Click on the **Remote** tab.

4. Enable **Allow remote connection to this computer** under the label **Remote Desktop.**

5. Deselect - if enabled - the **Only allow connections from computers running Remote Desktop with Network-level authentication (recommended)**, **only if there are computers on the network running older versions of Windows 10.**

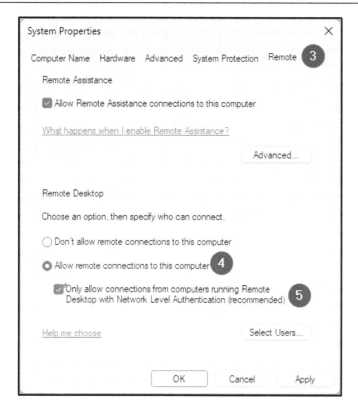

How to connect to a PC using Remote Desktop Connection

Remote Desktop Connection allows you to control a PC remotely in a completely autonomous way, providing 100% control of the PC to which you connect. Compared to remote control programs that replicate screen, keyboard and mouse, Microsoft Remote Desktop creates a true user session and disconnects anyone physically connected to the PC, ensuring your privacy.

1. Type **Remote Desktop Connection** in the search bar.

2. Enter the IP address or name of the PC you are connecting to.

3. Log in with your username and password.

You can also start Remote Desktop by typing the `mstsc` command in the Run window.

How to fix the CredSSP Encryption Authentication Error

Problem

The May 2018 Windows 10 update introduced security measures to address a vulnerability known as **CredSSP**. This can cause an error (typically connecting to a remote PC with Windows Server 2012 installed) like this:

Solution

The problem is in the client trying to connect. Thus, no changes are required on the remote server. In order to bypass this security measure it is necessary to modify parameters within the Local Group Policy Window Tool, which defines security parameters in the Pro operating systems, Enterprise and Education.

1. Type **gpedit.msc** in the search field on the taskbar. This will open the *Local Group Policy Editor* console.
2. Follow the path: Computer Configuration > Administrative Templates > System > Credentials Delegation.

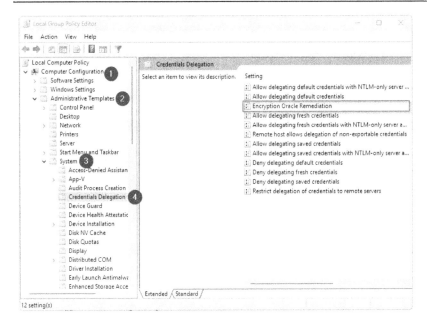

3. Click on **Encryption Oracle Remediation**.
4. Choose the **Enabled** option.
5. Set the **protection level** to **Vulnerable**.

Windows doesn't detect any PS/2 type keyboard or mouse

Windows 11 may have problems recognizing PS/2 devices, such as keyboards and mice, that do not use the USB port but the old standard port. This problem can occur either after a new installation of the operating system or after an upgrade. To fix it, just change a key in the registry.

Temporarily, you will need to use a USB keyboard and mouse to interact with your PC. PS/2 devices are managed by the **i8042prt** service, which controls the connection port. The cause of the problem may be an installation using USB devices or a corruption of settings. Both cases may have disabled the communication driver to avoid conflicts between PS/2 and USB. The registry key allows you to reactivate the i8042prt driver.

PS/2 type connection ports.

1. Open the Registry Editor (type REGEDIT in the Search field)
2. Navigate into

   HKEY_LOCAL_MACHINE\SYSTEM\CurrentControlSet\Servic es\i8042prt

3. Edit the value StartValue to 1 and click OK.

4. In case it does not exist, create a new 32-bit DWORD numeric value:

a. Do right click in a blank area and choose **New >
    DWORD 32 Bit value.**

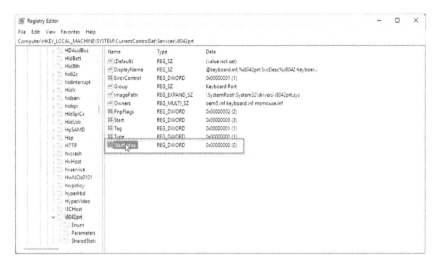

5. **Restart the computer by unplugging all USB
    keyboards and mice and leaving only the PS/2 devices
    connected.**

Be Careful!

Since Windows automatically disables PS/2 ports whenever USB keyboards
and mice are connected, it is recommended not to connect them anymore
and leave only the PS/2 peripherals. Otherwise, you will have to repeat the
operation.

If the mouse still does not work

1. Navigate to
    `HKEY_LOCAL_MACHINE\SYSTEM\CurrentControlSet\Servic
    es\mouhid`

2. Edit the value **Startvalue** to 1.

3. Restart the computer by unplugging all USB keyboards and
    mice and leaving only the PS/2 devices connected.

An alternative might be to purchase an adapter.

Lsass.exe takes up too many resources

Windows 11 has processes that can be quite cumbersome for some PCs. **Lsass** is a system process, the **Local Security Authority Subsystem Service**. However, the original executable itself is not the problem. It might slightly slow down your system, but it shouldn't consume all of its resources. If it causes excessive disturbance, it may also be a **malware**. There is malware that pretends to be this program but is started from other parts of the system disk. Therefore, perform thorough antivirus scans and check the file path via the Task Manager.

1. Go to the **Details** tab and right-click for each open lsass.exe.
2. Click on **Open file location**. The authentic path of **lsass.exe** is generally `C:\WINDOWS\SYSTEM32`.

> Warning: the malicious file may also mask as ISASS (or similar names) instead of LSASS. In the worst case, it may have modified the original program. To do this, it attempts an antivirus scan even directly on the file.

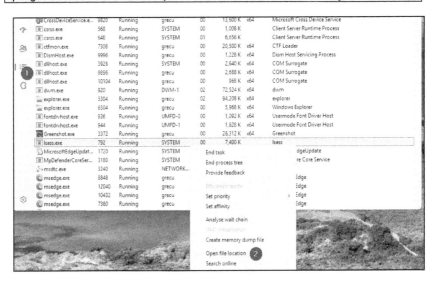

How to re-enable an audio device

I have often solved this problem simply by re-enabling the playback device, which was often disabled without an apparent reason.

Problem

By mistake or for no reason, an audio device was disabled

Solution

1. Search for Control Panel in the Taskbar Search field.
2. Set View by to Large Icons.
3. Click on Sound.

4. Right-click in the area where the playback devices usually appear and enable Show Disabled Devices and Show Disconnected Devices.

5. If there is a disabled device and you suspect it is the one that should be working, right-click on it and click on Enable.

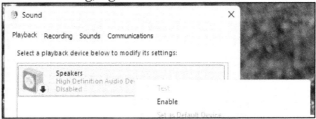

6. Test by playing a song or any audio. To ensure that the selected device is always used – in case it continues not to work – click on Set as Default Device after enabling it in the context menu as shown in the image

If there are no disabled or disconnected devices, it could be a driver-related issue. The drivers may have been uninstalled or never installed in the first place. Drivers can also become corrupted or, after an update, may no longer be compatible with your PC. Download the latest versions from the manufacturer's website to resolve the issue.

Security

How to disable real-time protection

Windows 11 includes real-time protection that scans every processed file, ensuring that any malicious elements are reported. It may be necessary to deactivate it in special cases, such as to intercept false positives.

> **Warning**
> Shutting down the protection will put your PC at high risk. Therefore, do this if it is strictly necessary and disconnect the computer from the internet whenever possible.

1. Open Settings.
2. On the left, click on Privacy & Security.
3. Click on Windows Security.

4. Click on Virus & threat protection.

5. Click on Manage settings.

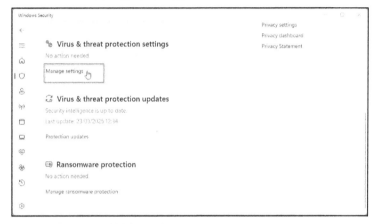

6. Set Real-time protection to Off.

This procedure is only valid if the installed antivirus is Microsoft's Windows Defender. If you have installed a third-party protection, please refer to the manufacturer's website.

How to disable Windows Firewall

Windows Firewall is an integrated protection feature in Windows. It is used to control incoming and outgoing traffic, attempting to block the passage of harmful information to the PC. However, it may be disruptive, and it might be necessary to temporarily disable it to rule it out as the cause, for example, of network software that isn't working.

> Warning: disabling a protection is always a risk factor. Only keep the Firewall disabled for as long as absolutely necessary and, if possible, do not surf the Internet.

1. Open Settings.
2. On the left, click on **Privacy & Security**.
3. Click on **Windows Security**.
4. Click on **Firewall & network protection**.

5. Click on the type of network currently active (for example Private Network).

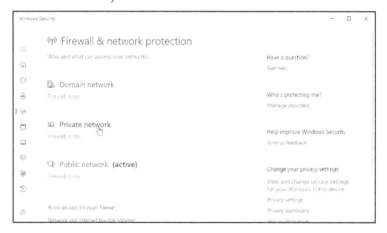

6. Toggle **Microsoft Defender Firewall** to **Off**.

7. Confirm the action (you must be an administrator user to do this).

8. To reactivate the firewall, follow the same steps again.

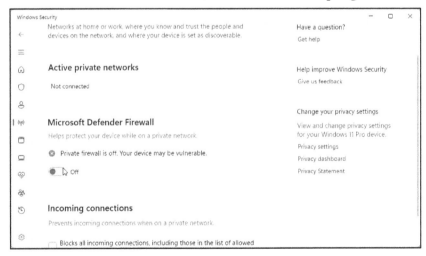

How to add an exception to Windows Firewall

The firewall, once disabled, opens doors to all incoming and outgoing traffic. If you have followed the previous guide and noticed that the problem was a port or program blocked by the firewall, you do not need to disable it permanently. You just need to add an exception, that is, open a connection port or unblock traffic to a particular program.

1. On the Search field in the taskbar, search for Windows Defender Firewall and click on the Windows Defender Firewall with Advanced Security.

2. You will find two types of rules:

   ▶ **Incoming connection rules:** all network traffic to the PC.

   ▶ **Outbound connection rules:** all traffic from the PC to the network.

   The configuration procedure is identical for both categories.

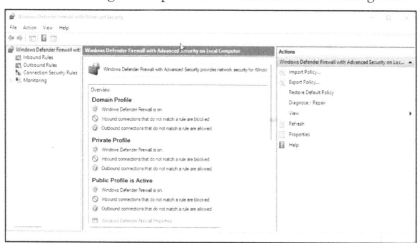

3. After selecting inbound or outbound, inside the Actions panel, on the left, click on New Rule...

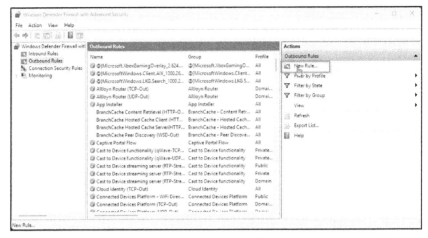

4. In the first step, you are asked to choose between an exception for a Port or a Program. The first opens a connection port (e.g., port 80 is dedicated to web pages, turning your PC into a navigable website at `http://ipaddress:80`; port 80 can be omitted since it's the standard port), while the second grants unrestricted inbound and outbound access to a specific program.

   ▶ **Port:** select the protocol type (TCP/UDP) and enter one or more ports.

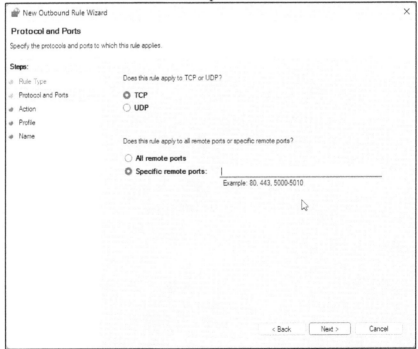

   ▶ **Program:** enter the path of the executable file.

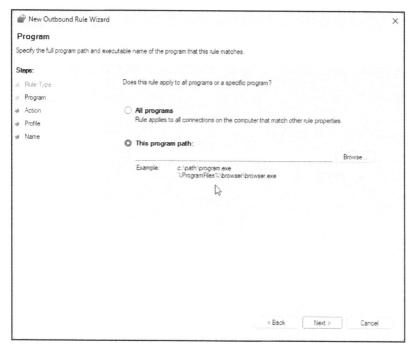

5. Choose whether to allow or block execution. The firewall opening exception is one where you **allow** traffic. The closing one is the one in which all traffic is **blocked** to/from that port or program.

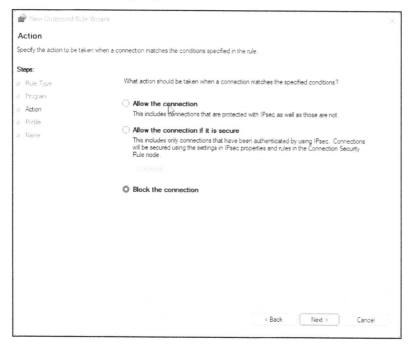

6. Choose the type of network in which the rule should operate (public, private or domain).
7. Give the rule a name and, if you want, a description.

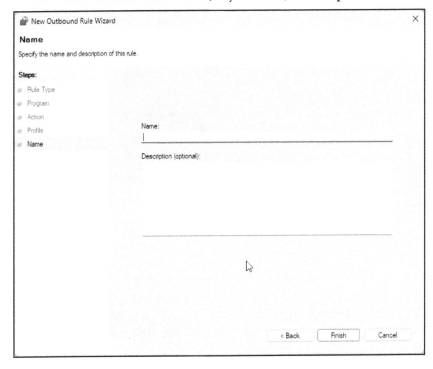

How to manage storage space with Storage Sense

Storage Sense is a feature designed to automatically free up disk space by removing unnecessary files without having to clean up your PC manually. It's ideal if you have little space available or want to keep the system always optimized.

1. Open Settings.
2. Click on **System** from the left menu.
3. Click on **Storage**.
4. Toggle **Storage Sense** to On.

Clicking directly on Storage Sense you can manage its settings.

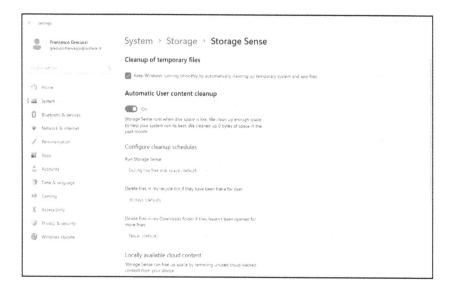

You can adjust the running frequency of Memory Sensor if you automatically delete items from the trash and downloads that have not been opened. In addition, by clicking on Run **Storage Sense** now you can start the procedure manually.

Tips for developers

How to enable Developer Mode

If this feature was not enabled, developers would not be allowed to launch their apps on their computers for testing, since Windows 11 blocks launching universal apps (not desktop programs, which are safe) unless downloaded from the Windows Store. This mode also allows you to activate other extra functions.

1. Open Settings.
2. On the left, click on System.
3. Scroll down to For Developers.
4. Set Developer Mode to On.
5. Confirm the activation of the mode by clicking on Yes.

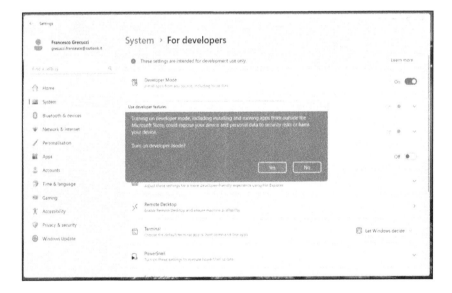

How to add a new environment variable

Environment variables are values loaded when the operating system starts. The most important variable is the **Path** array, which contains the directories related to command prompt executions.

For example, if I have a set of command-line tools in C:\Program Files\CommandList, *I would need to type* C:\Program Files\CommandList\commandname *every time or navigate to the directory using cd* C:\Program Files\CommandList.

With the **Path** variable, I can add this folder to the predefined directories and access the applications inside it simply by typing their name, as if they were basic commands—for example, commandname.

1. Open Settings.
2. On the left, click on System.
3. Scroll down to About.
4. Under the related links section, click Advanced system settings.
5. Click on Environment Variables.

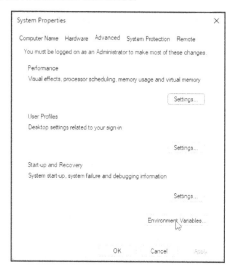

6. To add a new user or system variable, click the New... button.

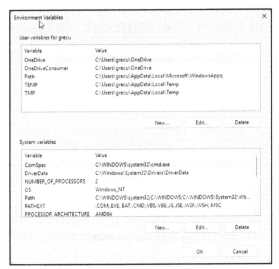

7. If the Path variable is the one you want to edit, select it and click **Edit...**

8. To add a new item to the list click on **New** and type in the path or click **Browse** to browse your PC folders.

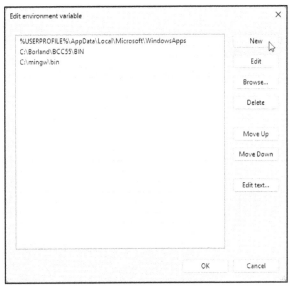

Edit source files with Visual Studio Code

This program is not included in Windows, but I find it very useful for those who want to combine the experience of Visual Studio with a powerful text editor. Lightweight and written in JavaScript, it allows you to write and edit code in various languages and formats, including: Batch, C, C#, C++, CSS, Clojure, CoffeeScript, Diff, Dockerfile, F#, Git Commit, Git Rebase, Go, Groovy, HLSL, HTML, Handlebars, Ignore, Ini, JSON, JSON with comments, Java, JavaScript, JavaScript React, Less, Lua, Makefile, Markdown, Objective-C, Objective-C++, PHP, Perl, PowerShell, Properties, Pug, Python, R, Razor, Ruby, Rust, SCSS, SQL, ShaderLab, Shell Script, Swift, plain text, TypeScript, TypeScript React, Visual Basic, XML, XSL, YAML e Log.

And if these languages weren't enough, there is the VS Code Marketplace, where you can find extensions and plugins for the Microsoft application.

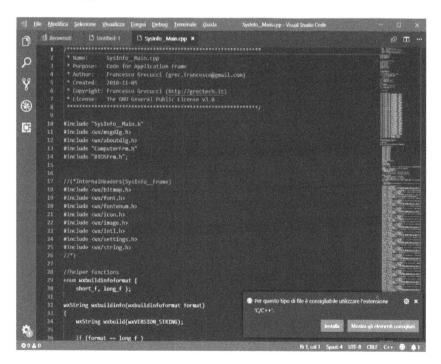

Windows PowerShell

Windows PowerShell is a command-line shell (also commonly called Terminal) and scripting language developed by Microsoft for task automation and system management.

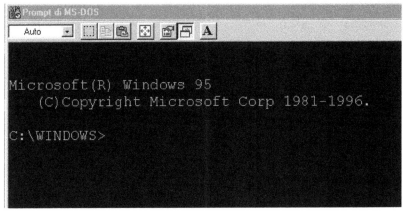

35 Windows 95 Command Prompt

It is more powerful than the Windows Command Prompt, because it allows you to run complex scripts and offers a wide range of cmdlets (commands) for managing various aspects of your operating system.

The old PCs had only a command prompt, no graphical interface. It was possible to start programs, manage files and folders, connect to the local network and do many other operations simply with a white on black (or sometimes green on black) command list. Microsoft operating systems based exclusively on character-based interfaces were called MS-DOS.

Nowadays, Powershell can be used for advanced operations on your PC and has a basic set of commands that we will look at in this book.

To open Powershell you just need to open the power user menu (Windows + X or right click on start button), and click on Terminal.

How PowerShell is made

Just like the command prompt, Powershell opens in a default folder, usually your user folder. From here, you can then navigate to different directories on the computer.

A **directory** is a container used to organize files and other directories in a file system. It is similar to a folder in which you can store different documents. Directories help keep the file system structured and make it easier to navigate and manage files. Directories keep the file system organized, simplifying navigation and file management.

A **path** is a text string indicating the location of a file or directory within a file system.

An example of a path is `C:\Users\Philip\`

List the contents of a directory

With the dir command you can list everything that is present in a directory, just type **dir** and press ENTER.

```
Windows PowerShell       ×    + ∨                                      —   □   ×

    Directory: C:\Users\Francesco

Mode                LastWriteTime         Length Name
----                -------------         ------ ----
d-----        28/01/2024     20:47               .android
d-----        17/09/2022     18:40               .dotnet
d-----        02/01/2023     21:51               .expo
d-----        16/11/2024     16:59               .nuget
d-----        15/09/2024     16:05               .ssh
d-----        17/09/2022     18:43               .templateengine
d-----        07/02/2023     22:22               .vscode
d-----        29/11/2022     21:55               Application Data
d-----        06/11/2022     15:15               Autodesk
d-r---        17/09/2022     18:39               Documents
d-----        04/03/2023     19:41               Graphisoft
d-r---        20/03/2023     22:37               OneDrive
d-----        17/09/2022     12:21               OpenVPN
d-----        17/09/2022     18:57               source
d-----        02/01/2023     21:51               test
-a----        28/11/2022     21:11          194  .gitconfig
-a----        18/11/2024     23:14        50827  43.png
-a----        18/11/2024     23:19        75985  4x3.png
-a----        18/11/2024     22:10         1237  particolare piastra alto.png
-a----        16/11/2024     16:30         2985  regwizard.log
-a----        16/11/2024     16:31        25478  sanct.log


PS C:\Users\Francesco>
```

Go to previous folder

If you are in the following path C:\Users\Philip\Pictures and you want to return to the folder C:\Users\Philip you just need to type the command
cd .. CD stands for Change Directory and serves to position itself within the folders that make up the system.

Enter a subfolder

To enter a subfolder use the command **cd foldername**

Enter a specific folder

Type the `cd` command followed by the path, for example `cd C:\Users\Laura\Downloads`

Change disk drive

You cannot type to enter another disk drive `cd D:` but you have to digit D: and then `cd D:\name`.

Create a folder

To create a folder in Powershell type this command
`New-Item –Path "newfolderpath" -ItemType "Directory"`

For example:
`New-Item -Path "C:\Users\Philip\Artworks" -ItemType "Directory"`

Other commands

Command	Feature	Example
Get-Help	Display a command's help	Get-Help Get-Process
Get-Process	Lists running processes	Get-Process
Get-Service	List available services	Get-Service
Start-Service	Start a service	Start-Service -Name "nomeservizio"
Stop-Service	Stop a service	Stop-Service -Name "nomeservizio"
Copy-Item	Copy a file or directory	Copy-Item -Path "C:\file.txt" - Destination "C:\backup\file.txt"

Move-Item	Move a file or directory	Move-Item -Path "C:\file.txt" - Destination "C:\documents\file.txt"
Remove-Item	Delete a file or directory	Remove-Item -Path "C:\file.txt"
Cls	Cleans the console screen	cls

Recovery Mode

How to enter recovery mode at boot

Windows 11's recovery mode allows you to take advantage of several repair tools, including the built-in formatting in your operating system. **Unfortunately, the F8 button when booting your PC is no longer the shortcut for starting emergency tools as in old versions of the operating system.**

From Settings

1. Open Settings.
2. On the left click on System.
3. Click on Recovery.
4. In the Advanced startup section click on Restart Now.

5. To enter Safe Mode, after restarting the PC on the screen, go to Troubleshoot > Advanced Options > Startup Settings > Reboot.
6. Choose one of the available start modes.

From the Login Screen

1. Inside the login screen, hold down the Shift key on your keyboard click on the ⏻ button, then click on the Restart button.
2. Repeat points 5, 6 of the preceding paragraph.

If Windows does not start and therefore does not get to the login screen, you will need to use the installation media or the recovery flash drive to get the recovery options.

Pressing the F11 key during startup

The validity of this procedure may be subject to change based on the PC manufacturer.

*   Press and hold the F11 button as soon as you turn on your PC

Repair corrupted system files

Windows allows you to repair corrupted system files with two frequently used commands in case of system problems.

Repair the system with the sfc tool

The **sfc /scannow** command allows you to scan and repair corrupted system files.

1. Open the Power User Menu (Windows + X key combination or right-click on start button).
2. Click on Terminal (Admin).
3. Type **sfc /scannow** and press Enter on the keyboard

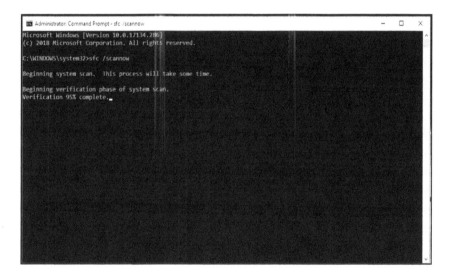

It may take some time to repair the entire system.

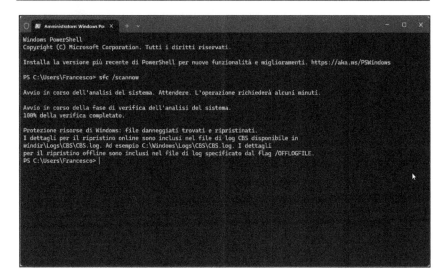

Once finished the prompt will tell if there are restored files as in the case of the screenshot above. The `C:\Windows\Logs\CBS\CGS.log` file records all the restoration operations carried out during the procedure.

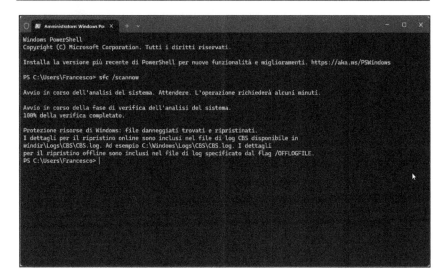

System recovery with DISM

With the DISM command you can repair corrupted system files, manage features and packages, and perform updates. One of the most widely used syntax is DISM /Online /Cleanup-Image /RestoreHealth. It allows you to restore the health of the current operating system by correcting any errors. This tool is essential to keep Windows efficient and fix problems that could compromise the stability and security of your operating system.

1. Open Power User Menu (Win + X).
2. Click on Terminal (Admin).
3. Write   DISM   /Online   /Cleanup-Image /RestoreHealth and press ENTER.

Again, the operation will take several minutes to complete.

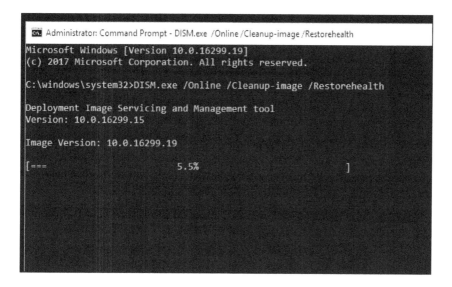

Tips & Tricks

Tips and tricks for those who do not want to waste time

Tips & Tricks

How to access over 200 system settings with GodMode

GodMode is a special folder that gathers more than 200 Windows settings. You need a few clicks to activate it. It groups together most of the settings, including many that are difficult to access with traditional controls. It's all sorted and categorized. You can drag it to your desktop, hard drive or personal folder.

> I remind you that most of these parameters must be set with administrator rights.

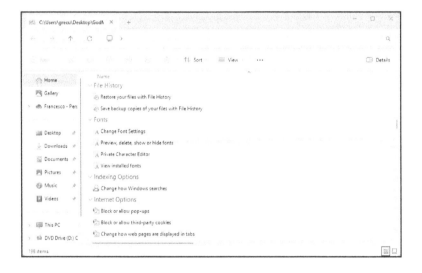

How to create the GodMode folder

1. Create a folder.
2. Name it `GodMode.{ED7BA470-8E54-465E-825C-99712043E01C}`
3. Click twice to open it.
4. To split into categories, right click on the folder and choose Sort> Application.

How to delete a file or folder without moving it to the trash

Some time ago I had to delete a few unnecessary files from my SSD. Since its capacity is only 250GB, I had to do some cleaning. I found several large files. Just moving them to the recycle bin would have wasted a lot of time. The result? Go to bed at 2.00 without having concluded anything. So, I thought "why not delete them directly without going through the intermediate step of the basket? I do not need to keep them: I am determined to delete them and I do not need a second confirmation." Yes, because of course this deletion is permanent and irreversible.

1. Choose the file or folder you want to delete and press the following key combination: Shift + Del.
2. Windows will ask for a confirmation of the possible deletion. If the file or folder to be removed is very large, it may still take some time to get rid of it.

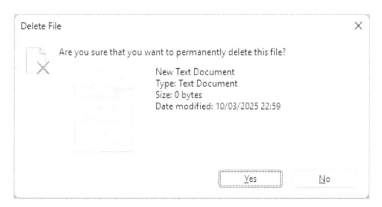

Warning: this procedure is very dangerous. It's like emptying the recycle bin: files are lost forever.

How to create a self-extracting/self-installing compressed file

If you have many items to send or upload on a website or server, very often you need to compress them into one file. A compressed archive is nothing more than a closed box containing files. In a nutshell, a file that compresses and contains one or more folders. You will only need to use a tool to open these boxes and that is a program like WinZIP.

Summary: compress data using one app into a single file, upload the compressed archive and extract it with another (or always the same) app. Windows, however, allows you to create a self-extracting archive, in a nutshell: an archive that extracts itself. In addition to the data, it includes a small decompression utility.

1. Search **Iexpress** in the taskbar Search field.
2. To generate the self-extracting archive choose the entry **Create new Self Extraction Directive File.**
3. You can choose the final result of the package:
    - Self-extracting archive in a temporary directory with automatic installation of a program
    - Self-extracting archive in a directory of your choice
    - .cab file.

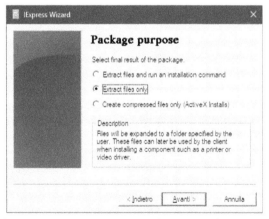

4. In the most common case, the second type (Extract files only) is chosen.
5. Give a name to the self-extracting package.
6. Enable user confirmation before extracting the archive, if needed.

7. Decide whether to include license terms to comply with.
8. Select the files to be included in the self-extracting archive.

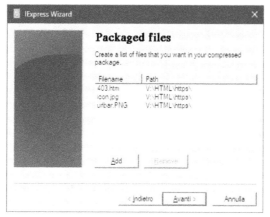

9. Choose the display style (I recommend Default).
10. Insert, if you wish, a message at the end of the program.
11. Enter the path and package name.
12. Confirm the use of the .SED file if you want to retrieve information to create other similar packages.
13. Click on **Next** to confirm the creation of the package.
14. Here it is!

Run the autoextract program

1. The compressed archive is in executable file, so it can be read by any Windows PC.
2. Choose the location where to save the files and click **OK**.

How to activate and use Clipboard History

Do you want to keep a history of your *Copy and Paste*? Simply enable the Clipboard History.

1. Open Settings.
2. Click on System in the left bar.
3. Click on Clipboard section.
4. Set Clipboard History to ON.

How to access the clipboard history

To view the clipboard history press Windows + V on your keyboard. A list of all recently copied items (text, images, links, etc.) will be shown.

If you have a Microsoft account, you can also sync your clipboard history across multiple devices.

How to disable "Do you want to turn on Sticky Keys?" popup

This guide is primarily for PC gamers and solves an annoying problem with the Permanent Keys feature introduced by Microsoft on Windows 95. This feature allows users with disabilities to activate accessibility features via the keyboard. If we don't need this feature, we can disable the permanent key activation message. Disabling this feature has become much easier with new versions of Windows.

1. Press the **SHIFT** button on your keyboard and wait for the Permanent Keys screen to open.
2. Click on Disable this keyboard shortcut in Ease of Access keyboard settings.

3. Enter in the Sticky Keys section and set Keyboard shortcut for sticky keys to Off.

How to have Emojis on hand

Emojis are everywhere. These cute pictograms of modern culture were introduced by Apple in 2008 (they already existed since the 90s as simple emoticons for mobile phones) and then extended to Android and its related mobile apps. Even Windows 11 allows you to place them anywhere: ☺ ☺ Of course, you need websites or apps that support this feature, such as WhatsApp Web, Facebook Messenger, etc.

1. Within a text field, press any of the **Windows + . (period)** keys. A screen will open containing all the emojis and also the animated GIFs.

Switch to another screen/projector with one click

For the versions of Windows from 7 onwards, thanks to the shortcut [Win + P] opens a quick menu for the management of two screens, useful especially for hasty and improvised connections to a projector, with different combinations of use:

- **PC screen only:** displays images at native resolution on the main PC screen;
- **Duplicate:** displays the same image on every screen at a common resolution for everyone.
- **Extend:** extends the desktop by using the other screens;
- **Second screen only:** turns the secondary projector/monitor into the single PC screen.

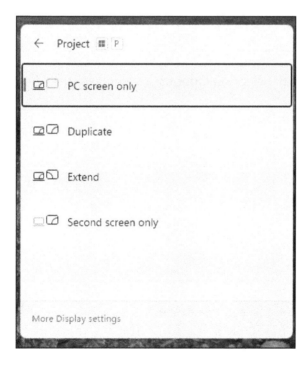

Show check boxes to select items in Windows Explorer

A more functional view to select items in a folder is the one that involves activating check boxes like those you see in this image:

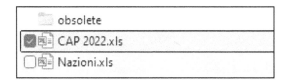

To activate them you will need only:

1. Go to File Explorer.
2. Click on the three dots.

3. Click on **Options**.

4. Select the tab **View**.
5. Scroll down to find and activate the option **Use Check Boxes to select items**.
6. Click on OK.

Microsoft PowerToys

Microsoft PowerToys is a set of small utilities for more experienced users, including:

- **Advanced Paste:** is a tool that lets you paste and convert text from the Clipboard to any format you need (for example, from text to HTML). It also has an artificial intelligence based option.

- **Always On Top:** allows you to fix one window in the foreground with a combination of keys Win + Ctrl + T.
- **PowerToys Awake:** Allows you to keep your PC active without having to change power and sleep settings. If you want your computer not to go into standby or shut down, you can turn on Awake and prevent this from happening.
- **Color Picker:** a perfect utility for graphic designers and web developers. Allows you to select colors anywhere on the screen and store their code in the clipboard. To open it you will just use the combination of keys Win + Maiusc + C.

- **Hosts File Editor:** a fast and easy editor to edit the file /etc/hosts with administrative rights.

- **Image Resizer**: an extension that allows you to quickly resize images. By right-clicking on File Explorer, you can instantly resize one or many images.

- **Mouse Without Borders**: allows you to interact with multiple computers from the same keyboard and mouse, easily sharing clipboard content between computers.

- **PowerRename**: allows bulk renaming, searching and replacing of file names.

- **Command not found**: it detects command-line errors (like "command not found") and suggests relevant WinGet packages to install, if available.

- **Quick accent**: is an easy way to write letters with accents, like on a smartphone.

These and many other utilities are available on PowerToys, you can download it at this link:
https://github.com/microsoft/PowerToys/releases/tag/v0.89.0

How to use the previous Task Manager Interface

The Task Manager in Windows 11 includes several improvements as well as a change to the graphical interface. If you prefer to use the Task Manager of Windows 10 with its functions organized in tabs and not in the sidebar there is a shortcut.

1. Type the command **taskmgr -d** in the Taskbar search field

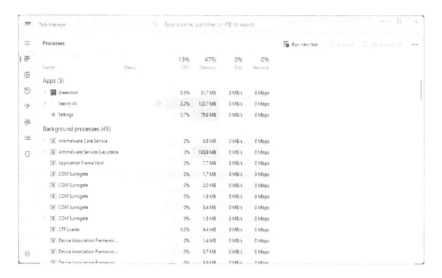

By creating a new link containing the command you can make the old task manager an icon.

1. Go to the Desktop.
2. Right-click on an empty area.
3. Click on New and select Shortcut.
4. Enter the command **taskmgr -d**.
5. Give the link a name.
6. You will have a new icon on your desktoP

FAQ

Frequently Asked Questions (FAQ)

Below are answers to questions that may be most common for Windows 11.

Can I install Windows 11 on a PC without the TPM 2.0 chip?

The answer is no. Or at least, not officially. Microsoft does not plan to install Windows 11 on PCs without the TPM 2.0, excluding a significant number of users from the transition to the new operating system.

However, there are various procedures available on the network to bypass system installation although these methods are not endorsed by Microsoft.

How much does it cost to upgrade to Windows 11 if I have Windows 10?

If your PC has an original Windows 10 license, the upgrade is free.

Which programs are compatible with Windows 11?

Generally, almost all programs compatible with Windows 10 are also compatible with 11. Windows 11 has the same structure as its predecessor with a new user interface.

Appendix A: Releases and Versions

Windows 11 Editions

Windows 11 targets different users. It is clear that the business features of the operating system will never be used in the home. To fit the pockets of all buyers, there are different versions as in previous products.

- **Windows 11 Home:** perfect for home users, includes all the basic features of Windows 11;
- **Windows 11 Pro:** designed for advanced users and businesses, offers additional features such as BitLocker, Hyper-V and Remote Desktop;
- **Windows 11 Pro Education:** similar to Windows 11 Pro, but designed for education;
- **Windows 11 Pro for Workstations:** designed for high-end workstations, includes advanced features such as support for multi-core processors and ECC memory;
- **Windows 11 Enterprise:** designed for large businesses, includes all the features of Windows 11 Pro plus advanced management and security features;
- **Windows 11 Education:** designed for educational environments, includes all the features of Windows 11 Pro;
- **Windows 11 IoT Enterprise:** designed for IoT (Internet of Things) devices, includes advanced security features and support for embedded devices.

Some of these versions may not be available for direct download from the Microsoft website but only through a commercial license or OEM (including purchase of a PC).

Comparation Table: Home & Pro Editions

Microsoft, on the official website https://www.microsoft.com/en-US/windows/compare-windows-11-home-vs-pro-versions?r=1, offers a comparison table between the home and small business users (Home) and business users (Pro), as shown below.

Home Vs Pro		
	Home	Pro
BitLocker Encryption		✓
Device Encryption	✓	✓
Find My Device	✓	✓
Firewall and Network Protection	✓	✓
Internet Protection	✓	✓
Parental Controls and Protection	✓	✓
Secure Boot	✓	✓
Windows Hello	✓	✓
Windows Information Protection (WIP)		✓
Windows Security	✓	✓
Remote Connection		✓
Remote Desktop Mode		✓
Kiosk Mode		✓
Active Directory Domain Join Support		✓
Hardware Virtualization		✓
Local Group Policy		✓

Windows 11 Releases

The important updates of Windows 11 released periodically are called *release*. Each release is in effect a new version of the operating system, with a release date and an end-of-support date.

Release	Build	Release	End of support
Windows 11 21H2	22000	2021	2024
Windows 11 22H2	22621	2022	2024
Windows 11 23H2	22631	2023	2025
Windows 11 24H2	26100	2024	2026

A bit of history

In this appendix we go back a bit on the history of Windows. In 1985, the demand for a user-friendly operating system was growing thanks to the introduction of Apple's Macintosh in the previous year. This was among the few that had, at the time, the **Graphical Interface** (GUI).

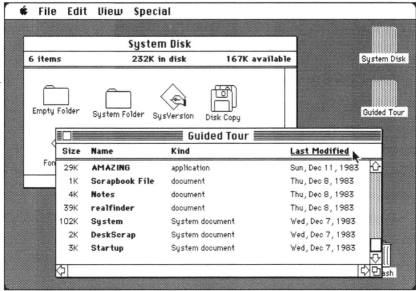

80s Apple System Software installed on Macintosh

Other operating systems such as AmigaOS also had this kind of visual design, although they were spartan, they helped make computers accessible to less experienced users. Before then, interfaces were text-based only. There was no mouse and you typed commands waiting for a response from the computer.

```
MS-DOS version 1.25
Copyright 1981,82 Microsoft, Inc.


The CDP Personal Computer DOS
Version 2.11 (C)Copyright Columbia Data Products, Inc. 1982, 1983
Current date is Tue  1-01-1980
Enter new date:
Current time is  0:00:06.15
Enter new time:

A:_
```

Microsoft was stuck on its MS-DOS, widely recognized and used worldwide (almost, but not so much, as Windows in our days) and had the need to develop its graphical interface. For this reason, Windows 1.0 was released. It was a graphical environment that extended MS-DOS with a very simple GUI.

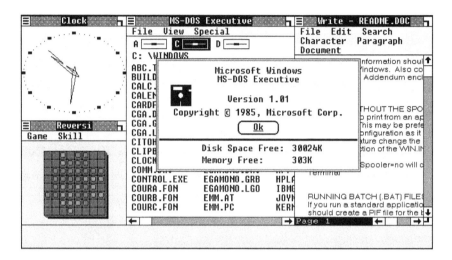

After some graphic interventions and several releases, we arrive at 1992 with Windows 3.1, well-suited for the 90s and destined for homes worldwide.

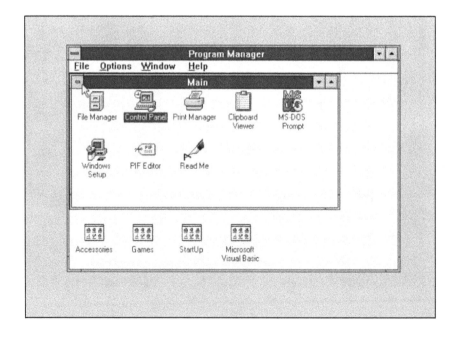

The revolution, however, came in 1995 with a milestone from Microsoft: Windows 95. Windows 95 was a huge commercial success, selling more than 7 million copies in the first five weeks of release. It was a turning point for the computer industry, with huge media and user attention for the new user interface and its advanced features. Windows 95 has introduced many of the features we take for granted in operating systems today, such as desktop icons, web browser integration, plug-and-play support, and more. It introduced a key feature: **Plug and Play**. It is a technology that automatically recognizes hardware devices when they are connected to the computer and configures them automatically, without the need for manual intervention by the user. Until then it was necessary to turn off the PC, connect the peripherals, install them manually, configure their parameters and pray that everything went well. Since the invention of Plug and Play, many technicians could finally sleep better at night.

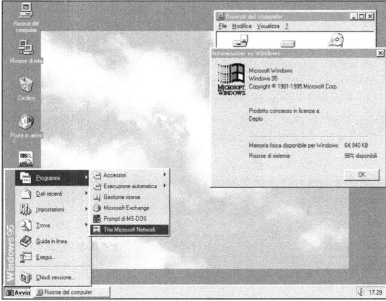

Windows 95

Since that year the implementations have been more and more, as shown in the table below, culminating in 2002 with the launch of what many consider the best Windows ever: Windows XP.

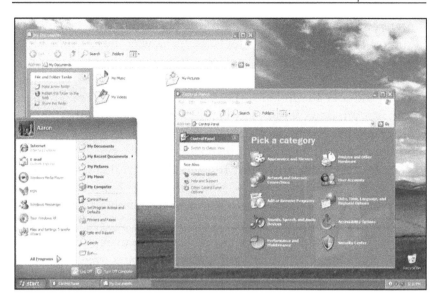

In these years of technological development, Microsoft has also made mistakes. An example is the three OS Windows ME, Windows Vista and Windows 8. All three are known for their bugs and commercial failures caused by various factors Windows 8 was so widely criticized and was full of problems for end users that Microsoft was forced to release a later version only one year later, 8.1, to fix the various issues. It is also worth noting that, thanks to faster internet connections and modern release and versioning methods, it has become easier for software companies to address issues.

Windows Version	Release Date
Windows 1.0	**November 1985**
Windows 2.0	**December 1987**
Windows 3.0	**May 1990**
Windows 3.1	**April 1992**
Windows for Workgroups 3.1	October 1992
Windows NT 3.1	July 1993
Windows NT 3.5	September 1994
Windows NT 3.51	May 1995
Windows 95	**August 1995**
Windows NT 4.0	July 1996
Windows 98	**June 1998**

Windows 2000	February 2000
Windows ME	**September 2000**
Windows XP	**October 2001**
Windows Server 2003	April 2003
Windows XP Professional x64 Edition	April 2005
Windows Vista	**January 2007**
Windows Server 2008	February 2008
Windows 7	**October 2009**
Windows Server 2008 R2	October 2009
Windows 8	**October 2012**
Windows Server 2012	September 2012
Windows 8.1	**October 2013**
Windows Server 2012 R2	October 2013
Windows 10	**July 2015**
Windows Server 2016	September 2016
Windows 10 November Update	November 2015
Windows 10 Anniversary Update	August 2016
Windows 10 Creators Update	April 2017
Windows 10 Fall Creators Update	October 2017
Windows 10 April 2018 Update	April 2018
Windows 10 October 2018 Update	October 2018
Windows 10 May 2019 Update	May 2019
Windows 10 November 2019 Update	November 2019
Windows 10 May 2020 Update	May 2020
Windows 10 October 2020 Update	October 2020
Windows 10 May 2021 Update	May 2021
Windows 11	**October 2021**

Appendix B:
keyboard shortcuts

Qui di seguito sono riportate le scorciatoie da tastiera direttamente dal sito web Microsoft: *https://support.microsoft.com/en-US/help/12445/windows-keyboard-shortcuts*

Keyboard Shortcuts

General

CTRL+X	Crop the selected item
CTRL+C o CTRL+INS	Copy the selected item
CTRL+V o SHIFT+INS	Paste the selected item
CTRL+Z	Cancel an action
ALT+TAB	Move between open apps
ALT+F4	Close the active item or exit the active app
WINDOWS +L	Lock your PC
WINDOWS+D	Show and hide the desktop
F2	Rename the selected item
F3	Search for a file or folder in File Explorer
F4	Display the address bar list in File Explorer
F5	Refresh the active window
F6	Scroll through screen elements in a window or on the desktop
F10	Activate the menu bar in the active app
ALT+F8	Show password on login screen
ALT+ESC	Scroll the items in the order they were opened
ALT+underlined letter	Execute the command associated with the letter
ALT+ENTER	Display properties for the selected item
ALT+SPACEBAR	Open the shortcut menu for the active window
ALT+LEFT arrow	Go back
ALT+RIGHT arrow	Go on

ALT+PGUP	Move back one screen
ALT+PGDOWN	Move forward a screen
CTRL+F4	Close the active document (in full screen apps that allow you to keep multiple documents open at the same time)
CTRL+A	Select all elements in a document or window
CTRL+D (o CANC)	Delete the selected item and move it to the Recycle Bin
CTRL+R (o F5)	Refresh the active window
CTRL+Y	Repeat an action
CTRL+RIGHT arrow	Move the cursor to the beginning of the next word
CTRL+LEFT arrow	Move the cursor to the beginning of the previous word
CTRL+DOWN arrow	Move the cursor to the beginning of the next paragraph
CTRL+UP arrow	Move the cursor to the beginning of the previous paragraph
CTRL+ALT+TAB	Use the arrow keys to switch between open apps
ALT+SHIFT+arrow keys	Move the focus of a group or pane in the Start menu to the specified direction
CTRL+SHIFT+arrow keys	Move the focus of a pane in the Start menu to another pane to create a folder
CTRL+arrow key (to move over an item)+SPACEBAR	Select multiple individual items in a window or on the desktop
CTRL+SHIFT with a direction key	Select a block of text
CTRL+ESC	Open the Start screen
CTRL+SHIFT+ESC	Open Task Manager
CTRL+SHIFT	Change keyboard layout if more than one is available

CTRL+SPACE BAR	Enable or disable Input Method Editor (IME) for Chinese
SHIFT+F10	Display the shortcut menu for the selected item
SHIFT with any arrow key	Select multiple items in a window or desktop, or select text in a document
SHIFT+CANC	Delete the selected item without first moving it to the Trash
RIGHT ARROW	Open the next menu on the right or open a submenu
LEFT arrow	Open the next menu on the left or close a submenu
ESC	Exit the current activity or stop it

Shortcuts with the Windows key

WINDOWS	Open or close the Start menu
WINDOWS+A	Open the Notification Center
WINDOWS+B	Set the focus in the notification area
Windows+SHIFT+C	PowerToys Color Picker
WINDOWS +D	Show and hide the desktop
WINDOWS +ALT+D	Display and hide the date and time on your desktop
WINDOWS +E	Open File Explorer
WINDOWS +F	Open Feedback Hub
WINDOWS +G	Open the game bar when a game is open
WINDOWS +H	Start dictation
WINDOWS +I	Open Settings
WINDOWS +K	Open Wireless Display Connect
WINDOWS +L	Lock your PC or change accounts
WINDOWS +M	Minimize all windows
WINDOWS +O	Lock the display orientation
WINDOWS +P	Switch display mode
WINDOWS +R	Open the Run dialog
WINDOWS +S	Open the search
WINDOWS +T	Swipe apps on the taskbar
WINDOWS +U	Open Accessibility Centre
WINDOWS +V	Scroll through notifications
WINDOWS +SHIFT+V	Scroll notifications in reverse order
WINDOWS +X	Open the Quick Link menu
WINDOWS +Z	Snap Layouts
WINDOWS + . or Windows + ;	Open the emoji panel

WINDOWS +,	Temporarily show the desktop
WINDOWS +PAUSE	Display the System Properties dialog box
WINDOWS +CTRL+F	Search for PCs (if you are online)
WINDOWS +SHIFT+M	Restore windows to desktop icon size
WINDOWS +number	Open the desktop and start the app added to the taskbar at the location indicated by the number. If the app is already running, switch to this app
WINDOWS +SHIFT+number	Open the desktop and start a new app instance added to the taskbar at the location indicated by the number
WINDOWS +CTRL+number	Open the desktop and go to the last active app window added to the taskbar at the location indicated by the number
WINDOWS +ALT+number	Open the desktop and open the Jump List for the app added to the taskbar at the location indicated by the number
WINDOWS +CTRL+SHIFT+number	Open the desktop and a new instance of the app that is in the specified location on the taskbar as administrator
WINDOWS +TAB	Open the task view
WINDOWS + UP arrow	Enlarge the window
WINDOWS + DOWN arrow	Remove the current app from the screen or minimize the desktop window
WINDOWS + LEFT arow	Enlarge the app or desktop window on the left side of the screen
WINDOWS + RIGHT arrow	Enlarge the app or desktop window on the right side of the screen
WINDOWS +HOME	Minimize all windows except the active desktop window (the second press will restore all windows)
WINDOWS +SHIFT+UP arrow	Enlarge the desktop window from top to bottom

WINDOWS +SHIFT+DOWN arrow	Restore/minimize active desktop windows vertically while keeping the width.
WINDOWS +SHIFT+LEFT or RIGHT arrow	Move an app or a desktop window from one monitor to another.
WINDOWS +SPACEBAR	Switch between input language and keyboard layout.
WINDOWS +CTRL+SPACEBAR	Switch to a previously selected input method.
WINDOWS +CTRL+ENTER	Open and enable the voice assistant
WINDOWS + +	Open the Magnifying glass
WINDOWS + /	Start the IME conversion
WINDOWS +CTRL+V	Open the audio mixer

Command Prompt

CTRL+C or (CTRL+INS)	Copy the selected text
CTRL+V or (SHIFT+INS)	Paste the selected text
CTRL+M	Activate mark mode
ALT+selection key	Start selection in block mode
Arrow keys	Move the cursor in the specified direction
PGUP	Move the cursor up by one page
PGDN	Move the cursor down by one page
CTRL+HOME (mark mode)	Move the cursor to the beginning of the buffer
CTRL+END (mark mode)	Move the cursor to the end of the buffer
CTRL+UP arrow	Move up one line in the output history
CTRL+DOWN arrow	Move down one line in the output history

| CTRL+HOME (history navigation) | If the command line is empty, move the view window to the top of the buffer. Otherwise, delete all characters to the left of the cursor in the command line. |
| CTRL+FINE (history navigation) | If the command line is empty, move the view window to the command line. Otherwise, delete all characters to the right of the cursor in the command line. |

Dialog Boxes

F4	Display items in the active list
CTRL+TAB	Move forward through tabs
CTRL+SHIFT+TAB	Move backward through tabs
CTRL+number(1-9)	Switch to the tab indicated by the number
TAB	Move forward through options
SHIFT+TAB	Move backward through options
ALT+underlined letter	Execute the command (or select the option) associated with the indicated letter
SPACEBAR	Select or deselect the checkbox if the active option is a checkbox
BACKSPACE	Open a folder one level up if a folder is selected in the Save As or Open dialog box
Arrow keys	Select a button if the active option is a group of radio buttons

File Explorer

ALT+D	Select the address bar
CTRL+E	Select the search box
CTRL+F	Select the search box
CTRL+N	Open a new window
CTRL+W	Close the active window
CTRL+mouse scroll	Change the size and appearance of file and folder icons
CTRL+SHIFT+E	Display all folders above the selected folder
CTRL+SHIFT+N	Create a new folder
NUM LOCK+asterisk (*)	Display all subfolders of the selected folder
NUM LOCK+plus sign (+)	Display the contents of the selected folder
NUM LOCK+minus sign (-)	Compress the selected folder
ALT+P	Display the preview pane
ALT+ENTER	Open the Properties dialog box for the selected item
ALT+RIGHT arrow	Display the next folder
ALT+UP arrow	Display the folder the selected folder was in
ALT+LEFT arrow	Display the previous folder
BACKSPACE	Display the previous folder
RIGHT arrow	Display the current selection (if collapsed) or select the first subfolder
LEFT arrow	Collapse the current selection (if expanded) or select the folder the selected folder was in
END	Display the bottom of the active window
HOME	Display the top of the active window
F11	Maximize or minimize the active window

Virtual Desktop

Tasto WINDOWS +TAB	Virtual Desktop Screen
Tasto WINDOWS +CTRL+D	Add a virtual desktop
Tasto WINDOWS +CTRL+RIGHT arrow	Switch between virtual desktops created on the right
Tasto WINDOWS +CTRL+LEFT arrow	Switch between virtual desktops created on the left
Tasto WINDOWS +CTRL+F4	Close the virtual desktop in use

Settings

WINDOWS +I	Open the settings
BACKSPACE	Return to the settings home page
Type on any page with the search box	Search for settings

Taskbar

SHIFT+click on a taskbar button	Open an app or quickly open another instance of an app
CTRL+SHIFT+click on a taskbar button	Open an app as an administrator
SHIFT+right-click on a taskbar button	Show the window menu for the app
SHIFT+right-click on a grouped taskbar button	Show the window menu for the group
CTRL+click on a grouped taskbar button	Scroll through the group windows

Analytical Index

Your Notepad

References

Bibliography

M.David Stone, Alfred Poor (2002) Troubleshooting Your PC

From the Web

Microsoft Support, *support.microsoft.com*
Microsoft TechNet, *technet.microsoft.com*
Wikipedia contributors. "Windows Registry." Wikipedia, The Free Encyclopedia. Wikipedia, The Free Encyclopedia, 7 Dec. 2018. Web. 26 Dec. 2018.